Markdown Dreams

How to do things with Markdown and Git

Peter S. Conrad

Markdown Dreams

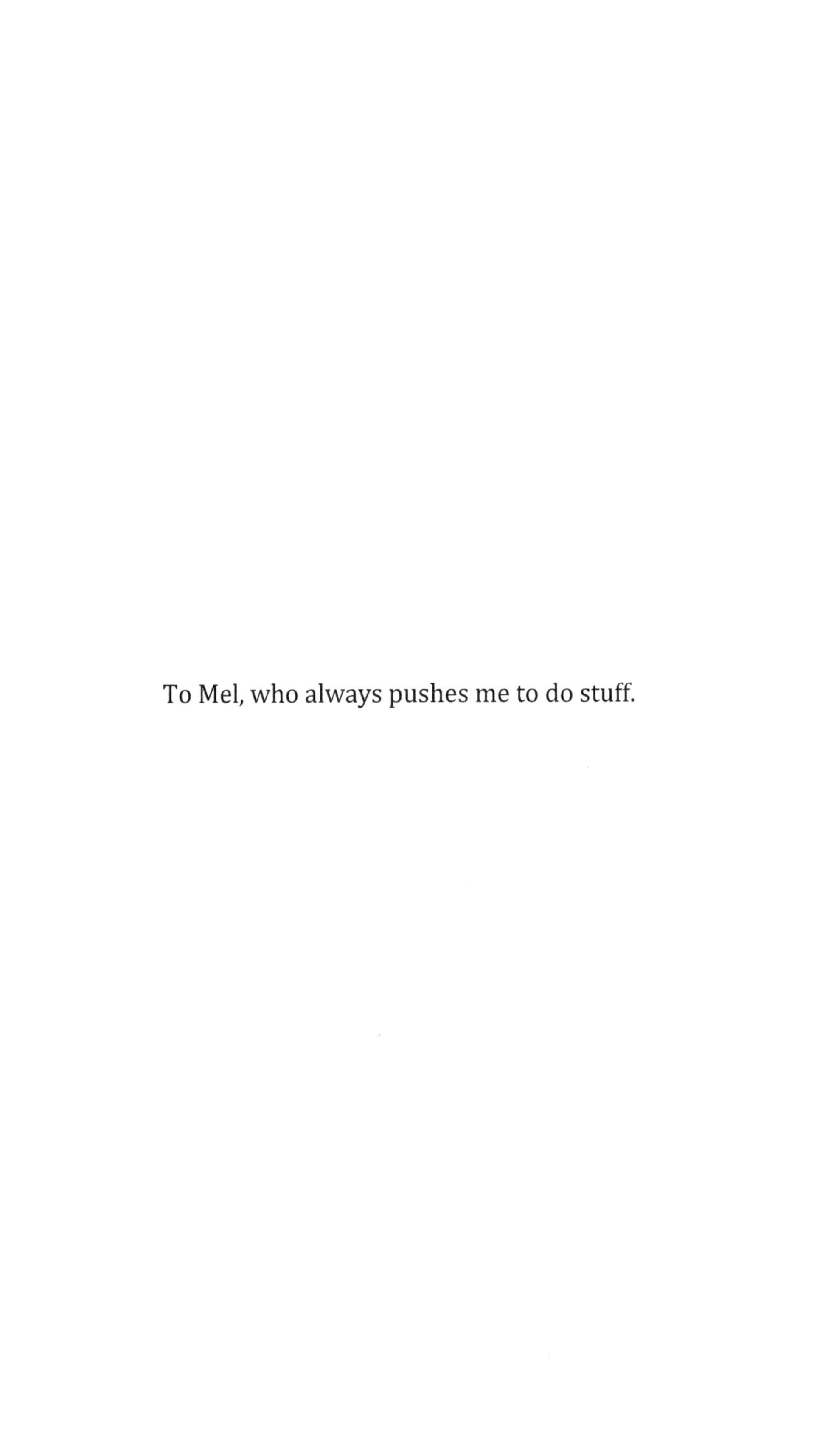

To Mel, who always pushes me to do stuff.

Contents

Introduction

In 2019, I was asked to put together a presentation covering the basics of Markdown syntax. I had worked with Markdown for a little while at a well-known social media company some years before, but I hadn't explored it too deeply.

I knew I needed to do some research.

That was the beginning of 18 months of deep Markdown spelunking. I explored the differences between different flavors and editors, various Markdown extensions, and a number of presentation and publishing tools. Along the way, I got better at Git, too, an excellent tool that used to fill me with dread. I changed jobs and was suddenly using Markdown and Git every day.

I presented a more detailed talk to a larger audience, and discovered that people are eager to learn more about Markdown. I thought it might be useful to write a simple book that would show a few of the tools that have become available.

I like Markdown a lot. I've learned a great deal about it and found a few tools I enjoy using. I take all my notes with Typora and Dropbox, and I write documentation day to day in Markdown using Sublime Text. I now use Git every day, not just at work but for personal projects. This book started as an MkDocs website that I edited in Ghostwriter and managed on GitHub—on a Raspberry Pi, no less.

Gradually, Markdown has become a tool I use in several different ways nearly every day. It's simple, runs on any platform, and works with a variety of tools. When I take notes in Markdown, I know I can easily turn them into a website, a slide presentation, or a book like this one.

This book shows how the big pieces fit together: what tools to use and a couple fairly simple Git workflows. There's much more to explore. Along the way, as you start with Hugo or Pandoc, or a tool that's not listed in the book, you'll find frustrations and epiphanies for sure. However, it is my hope that the recipes here will help you get over the initial conceptual hurdles more quickly—or even get you unstuck if you get into some Git trouble.

This is the book I wish I'd had when I started learning about Markdown. I hope it helps you to read it, as much as it has helped me to write it.

Peter Conrad

California, 2020

How to do things with Markdown

Markdown is not just a markup language. It is an ecosystem of powerful tools that lets you quickly craft an HTML page, manage a full doc set, take notes, write a novel—even create a slide presentation. Markdown makes it easy to create content quickly, because its simple syntax covers most of the bases without requiring you to take your fingers off the keys.

With shared storage or source control, Markdown can be a powerful collaboration framework, suitable for both technical and non-technical contributors and supported by tools that meet every preference.

This guide presents some basic recipes for working with some useful Markdown tools. Each recipe lists what you'll need. Read "Getting started" on page 5 to learn how to get set up.

If you want to know more about the available tools first, you can browse these sections:

- "Markdown editors" on page 9
- "Source control with Git" on page 16
- "Publishing tools" on page 43

Consider installing more than one Markdown editor to see which features you like.

About the recipes

Each recipe explains the goals, "ingredients," and procedures for an interesting way to use Markdown. Just as a lasagna recipe doesn't contain instructions for preheating (or installing) the oven, the recipes in this guide don't contain software installation instructions. Git commands are not repeated from recipe to recipe, but documented more centrally to keep the recipes short.

The idea is to help you get started and work around some of the less obvious "gotchas"—not to provide complete documentation. You might find it helpful to open each tool's website as you try the recipes, in case you get stuck.

Some recipes go together. You might use Centralized Git workflow to manage content you are editing in a Git wiki with the goal of publishing a website with Hugo. Or you might take content that you started by taking notes and turn it into a slide presentation.

Getting started

You can start working with Markdown just by opening your favorite text editor and starting to type—but you probably want to do more than that. For example, you might want to share information on a website or wiki, take notes, or publish an eBook. To get the most out of Markdown, you'll want to be familiar with some of these tools and topics.

Ingredients

These are the tools and resources you will use for the recipes in this guide.

Markdown editor	A Markdown editor is a specialized text editor that works with Markdown. Different editors have different features—you'll want to play with more than one to find out which ones you like.
Pandoc	Pandoc enables your Markdown editor to import and export in several formats and also has a few tricks of its own. I recommend Pandoc for anyone who works with Markdown.
Shared storage	If you are collaborating with others, you might need a shared place to store Markdown files. You might also want web hosting or a blogging platform where you can publish your content when it's complete.
Git	Source control can be very important for collaborating without catastrophe. You'll need an account with a Git host, a Git client, and Git installed on your computer.
Publishing tools	Documentation management tools, static site generators, and Pandoc can be useful to convert your content to a final format for general consumption.

You can install everything up front, or just install what you need as you go along. If you're not sure, start with the following steps:

1. Install Pandoc.
2. Choose and install a Markdown editor.
3. Set up Git.

HINT: Some editors detect Pandoc, so installing Pandoc first can make setup easier.

Things to know

You'll find it easiest to follow the recipes in this guide if you are comfortable with the following topics:

Markdown Syntax
Although some editors provide a WYSIWYG experience, knowing how to write Markdown directly will help you work more quickly and easily with a wider variety of tools.

- See "Markdown cheatsheet" on page 102

Markdown comes in a bunch of flavors with different capabilities:

- CommonMark
- GitHub Flavored Markdown (GFM)
- Markdown Extra
- MultiMarkdown (MMD)

Here are a few differences between these common flavors:

	CommonMark	GFM	Markdown Extra	MMD
Fenced Code Blocks	✓	✓	✓	✓
Syntax Highlighting		✓	✓	✓
Tables		✓	✓	✓
Footnotes			✓	✓
Auto-linking		✓		
Strikethrough		✓		
Definition Lists			✓	✓
Abbreviations			✓	✓

Some tools include extensions that provide additional capabilities. Hugo, for example, has an extensible framework of shortcodes that let you create your own features. Many tools, including MkDocs, use the Python-Markdown Extensions, which offer additional formatting capabilities out of the box. There are also more complex systems that work with Markdown, such as Markdown+Math, which displays LaTeX math, and Mermaid, which generates diagrams.

NOTE: Different tools offer different extensions, so plan ahead for the content you want to create. For example, some of the Markdown extensions available in MkDocs don't work in Pandoc, and vice versa.

The command line

Some of the recipes in this guide involve at least some typing on the command line. You'll definitely need to use the command line a little bit when you're working with Hugo, MkDocs, or Pandoc.

Working with a package manager

Installing some tools requires using one of the following common package managers:

- Linux: apt-get or yum
- macOS: Homebrew
- Windows: Chocolatey

A package manager can make it easy to install several packages at once. For example:

```
sudo apt-get install python3 ghostwriter pandoc mkdocs hugo
```

Git

Git is very powerful, but doesn't have to be hard to use. Some of the recipes in this book use Git, with an eye toward keeping things simple. If you already know Git, you can choose to do things differently. If you don't know git, take a look at "Source control with Git" on page 16.

Other documentation tools

The point of Markdown is to produce content that can be published and consumed in another format—originally HTML, and now Word, slides, PDF, and other formats. You should know something about tools like Acrobat, Google Drive, Microsoft Office, and other places where your Markdown might end up.

HINT: If you want to find more information about the tools and techniques in this book, check out "Links" on page 125.

Markdown editors

Markdown editors let you edit your content and often integrate with conversion and publishing tools. There are a few different types available:

- **Dedicated Markdown editors** let you write and edit Markdown code with syntax highlighting, and often have a preview pane or separate preview window.
- **Code editors**, designed for editing various kinds of source code, can be quite extensible and sophisticated, offering plugins and packages that provide many of the capabilities of a dedicated Markdown editor.
- **Text editors** are more general-purpose than dedicated Markdown editors, and may or may not offer Markdown syntax highlighing or preview.
- **Browser-based tools** range from simple Markdown preview tools to full-featured writing and publishing tools that integrate with source control, blogging, or collaboration websites.

For blogging, you can use a browser-based tool—in fact, some blogging sites support Markdown already. If you plan to create and manage documentation or other complex writing projects, it makes sense to install a dedicated Markdown editor. If you are adding Markdown to your code development environment, several code editors support Markdown very nicely.

Dedicated Markdown editors

Most dedicated editors are use syntax highlighting to make it easier to see that's going on.

Two tools in particular stand out:

- Joplin, a specialized editor for writing notes and to-do lists
- Typora, an elegant WYSIWYG editor for Markdown

Byword

macOS/iOS

Byword provides syntax highlighting and an in-app preview, letting you export to a few formats or publish directly to Medium, WordPress, Blogger, Tumblr, and Evernote.

Caret

macOS/Windows/Linux

Caret offers interesting features such as a folders/files view, multiple cursors, keyboard-based selection tools, and smart help with tables and other formatting features.

Ghostwriter

Windows/Linux

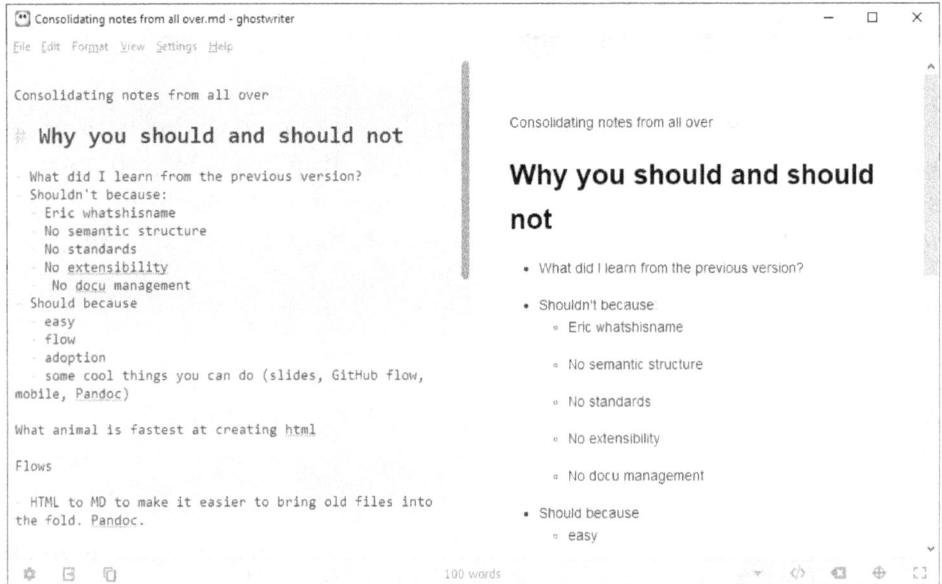

Ghostwriter is a free and open source split-screen editor that integrates with Pandoc and offers smaller "heads-up display" windows that provide document information and a Markdown cheat sheet.

iA Writer

macOS/iOS/Android/Windows

iA Writer is intended for writers who want to focus. It integrates with Dropbox and imports and exports to Microsoft Word.

Joplin

macOS/iOS/Android/Windows/Linux

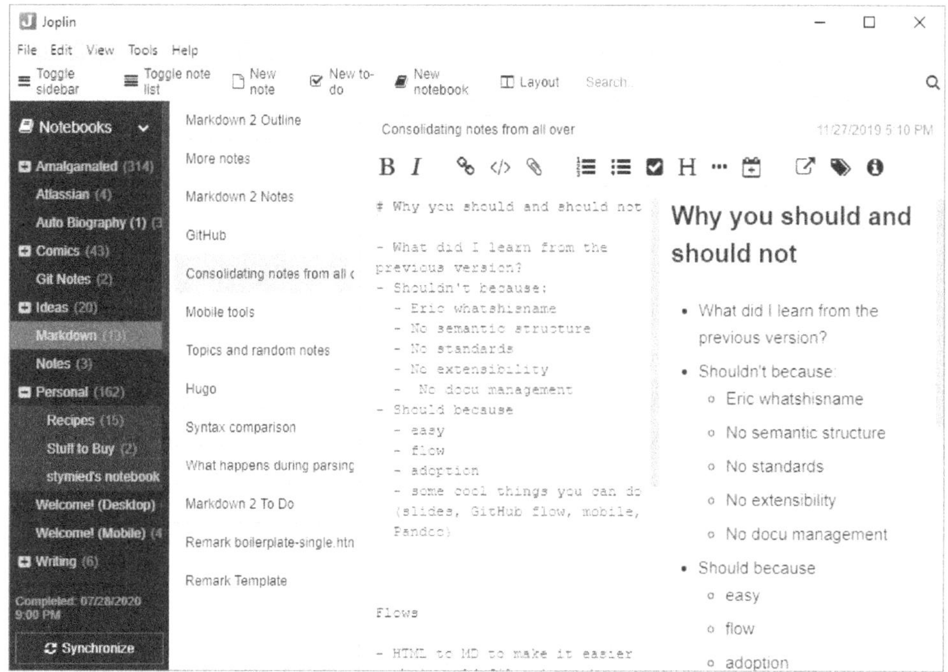

Joplin is an open-source note-taking and to-do application that syncs to DropBox, OneDrive, and other cloud storage. It includes an editor, but also supports the external editor of your choice. It offers end-to-end encryption and can import Evernote notebooks.

MacDown

macOS

MacDown is an open source Markdown editor with a split screen and live preview, inspired by an early Markdown editor called Mou.

Typora

macOS, Windows, Linux

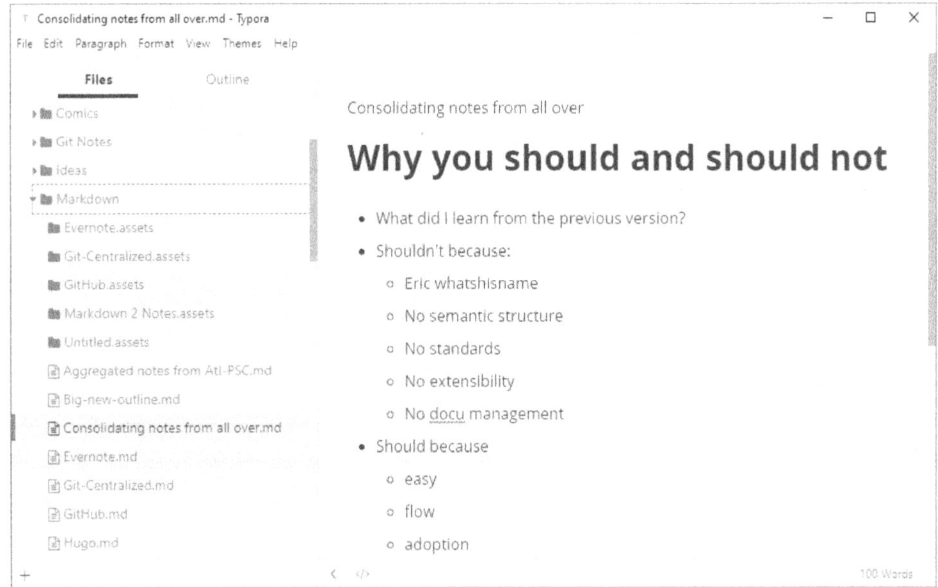

Typora is a Markdown editor that includes not only a syntax editing mode but a fully WYSIWYG editing experience. It integrates with Pandoc, so it can import and export a number of formats. Typora offers a files and folders view, which is helpful when working on longer documents or taking notes.

Code editors

If you are documenting code in a large organization, you might need to write Markdown that meets fairly stringent standards to work with your documentation management and publishing system. Code editors, while they are not designed specifically for Markdown, sometimes offer sophisticated packages to support Markdown editing and preview. An advantage of a code editor is the ability to do things like jump to a specific line number or set text wrapping rules. The following editors, among others, are worth a look:

- Atom
- Sublime Text
- Visual Studio Code

Text editors

Because Markdown is just plain text, even the simplest text editor can be a capable tool. Some well-established text editors offer Markdown modes:

- BbEdit
- Emacs
- Vim

Browser-based tools

Browser-based Markdown tools can be an easy, portable way to write Markdown that you intend to publish to a blog. Some integrate directly with Git hosts, blogging sites, or cloud storage.

Dillinger

Dillinger is an open source online Markdown editor that integrates with DropBox, GitHub, Google Drive, and OneDrive. You can also import from BitBucket, or upload Markdown and HTML files from your computer.

HackMD

HackMD is an online Markdown editor, free for personal use, that integrates with GitHub and includes tools for creating slides.

StackEdit

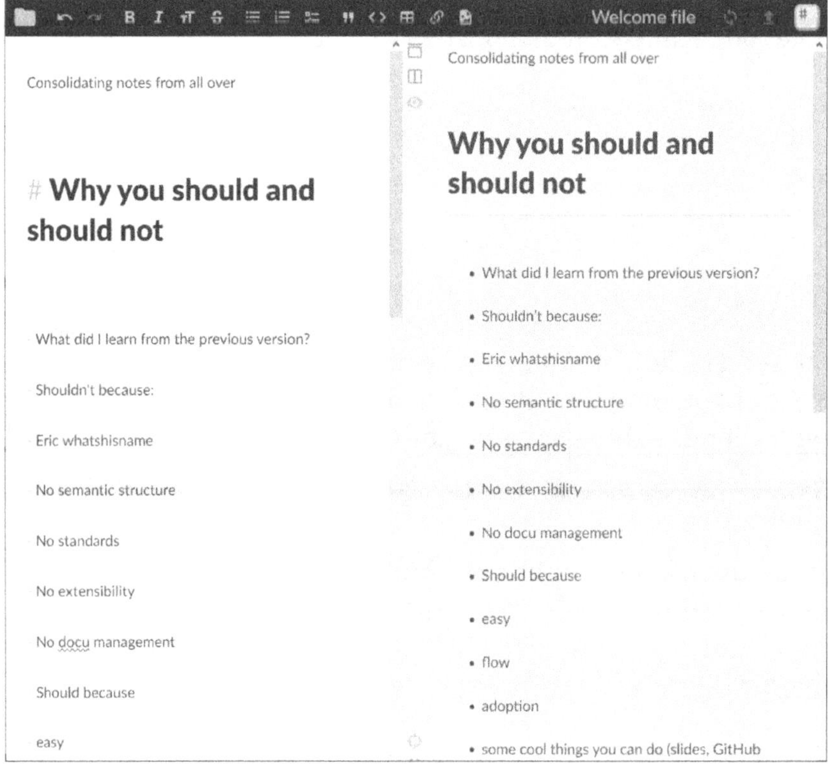

StackEdit is an online editor that syncs with DropBox, GitHub, GitLab, and Google Drive. You can import Markdown and HTML files, export with Pandoc, and publish to Blogger, Wordpress, and Zendesk.

Markdown Dingus

Markdown Dingus shows how John Gruber's official version of Markdown renders to HTML.

Babelmark

Babelmark is a useful tool for comparing the way different implementations and flavors render Markdown. If you are trying to figure out a problem with your Markdown, Babelmark can help.

Storage

The simplest place to store Markdown is on your own computer, of course. You can merrily save files to a folder deep in `My Documents` and go on your way, perhaps emailing someone a Pandoc-generated PDF from time to time. But if you want to enjoy the true power of collaborating and publishing with Markdown, you'll want to share the files you're working on or publish them in another form.

> HINT: Some Markdown tools, especially browser-based editors, sync directly with cloud storage and blogging sites.

A shared server

If you are collaborating on documents or contributing to documentation at work, you might need access to a shared server such as SharePoint or Samba, WebDAV, or online tools such as a Google Drive account. You can store your source files there or upload HTML, Word, PDF, and other documents you create from your Markdown.

Cloud storage

Cloud storage services like Box, DropBox, and OneDrive are a great place to keep documents you want available from everywhere. You can save Markdown files from one computer and have them available on other devices, even sharing them with colleagues. Cloud storage is great for taking notes, because you can work from anywhere.

Web hosting

If you're creating online documentation or a website, you'll need a place to host it. Web hosting is far too big a subject to cover here, but consider investigating whether you need any of the following:

- A blog service such as Wordpress, Blogger, or Medium
- A web host, to present your HTML files as web pages
- FTP software to upload HTML to a web host
- An integrated online publishing service or platform

Source control with Git

Any time you collaborate with others, source control is important. If you just share a folder in the cloud, eventually there will come a time when someone overwrites or deletes something important. That's where source control comes in. And by "source control," I mean Git.

NOTE: If you're just using Markdown to take notes or create Word documents, PDFs, and slides, you might not need Git. But if you're collaborating with others, read on!

With Git, you synchronize files on your computer with files on a remote repository—usually an online Git host.

Why Git?

Back in the day, there were all kinds of source control systems. The ones I remember were all pretty easy to use, but were all centralized—meaning that only one person could edit any given file at any given time. Worse, it meant that there was one central source of truth; if that were to be corrupted or lost, everything would be gone. Git solves these problems and doesn't have to be hard to use.

Get Git

You'll need a place to host a Git repository. You might start by signing up with a Git host. Here are a few examples:

- Bitbucket
- GitHub
- GitLab

You can use Git on the command line, but it's even easier if you use a Git client. For example:

- GitHub Desktop
- Sourcetree

HINT: While any Git client should work with any Git host, it's not a bad idea to use the client and host that go together. For example:

- Bitbucket and Sourcetree
- GitHub and GitHub Desktop

This guide includes instructions for these two combinations.

Git concepts

Git is different from older source control systems. A lot of things that used to be intuitive—like the idea that we're working on *files* and we need to *lock* them so that someone else can't *check them out* from the *central repository*—have no currency in the Git world:

- There's no *central repository.* A central repository would represent both a bottleneck and a single point of failure, so why do it?
- No one *checks out* files because there's no central repository.
- We don't need to *lock* files because we don't have to worry about them being *checked out.*

In fact, Git doesn't care about *files* at all. Git only cares about *changes.*

There's a lot to know about Git. As a writer, you should be able to decide how much you want to learn. You might just want to learn *exactly* enough to do your writing and keep out of trouble. That's the goal here. If you want to learn more, check out The Git Book.

What things mean in Git

Here are a few basic Git terms you'll see in some of the recipes.

Commit

As you make changes to the files you're working on, saving periodically, you also tell Git from time to time that you want your changes tracked. This is called *committing* the changes, and is a little like "saving changes to Git." Git makes it easy by noticing the changes you've made so you can review them and make sure you're not accidentally tracking something irrelevant. When you commit, you type a little note describing the changes so that people know what you did.

A group of changes you've committed is also called a *commit.*

Stage

Before you commit changes, you tell Git which changes to track. This is called *staging.* Since changes go with files, sometimes people think of it as staging the files themselves—but it's really the changes that Git wants to know about. If you delete a file, that's a change too.

Repository

When you have committed, your changes are stored in the local *repository,* or *repo* for short. It's just like that old central repository, but it's on your computer.

Push

If you want other people to be able to work on your files, then you need to put them in an online repository (such as Bitbucket, GitHub, or GitLab). This is not *checking in* since the changes are already committed to your local repository. This is called a *push* to a *remote repository*.

Clone

Once something is in an online repository, an authorized person can *clone* their own copy of the whole repository and work on the files locally.

Pull

As you work on a repository you've cloned, you *pull* the latest changes from the remote repo to stay up to date.

Branch

Git lets people work in separate work streams called *branches* so that they don't interfere with each other's work. A branch is just a series of commits (and a commit is a group of changes). You're always working in a branch, even if there's only one branch. When you take turns working in different branches, Git remembers the state of everything in each branch so that when you switch between them everything is just how you expect it.

Creating a new branch is called *branching,* of course. The Git command for creating (or switching to) a branch is called, confusingly, *checkout.*

There are different branching strategies. Some are complicated; others are simple. The recipes in this guide use two simple branching strategies, described in "Git basics" on page24.

Merge

If there's more than one branch, there always comes a time to *merge,* which means to add the changes from one branch into another.

Why branching is cool

Git keeps track of the whole history of all the changes on all the branches. Not only does that mean you can roll back to any point in time, it also means that when you switch branches all your files magically change to match whatever changes you've made in that branch.

For example, I created a branch called `test-branch` based on the `master` branch. Working in `test-branch`, I added a file called `new-file.md` which you can see in the directory:

```
$ ls
getting-started  img  index.md new-file.md
```

When I switch to `master`, it's not there:

```
$ git checkout master
Switched to branch 'master'
Your branch is up to date with 'origin/master'.
$ ls
getting-started  img  index.md
```

When I switch back to `test-branch`, it's there:

```
$ git checkout test-branch
Switched to branch 'test-branch'
$ ls
getting-started  img  index.md  new-file.md
```

Branching is cool.

Git setup

If you want to be ready for all the recipes in this guide, follow these steps to install Git and a Git client, sign up for a host, and set up your first repository.

Install Git

On the command line, check whether Git is installed on your computer by typing:

```
git --version
```

If Git is not installed, follow these steps.

1. Install Git on your computer:
    - **Windows**: https://git-scm.com/download/win
    - **macOS**: https://git-scm.com/download/mac
    - **Linux**: https://git-scm.com/download/linux
2. Install a git client such as Sourcetree or GitHub Desktop.

HINT: You can use any Git client with any Git host, but some clients work especially well with specific hosts. For example:

- Sourcetree and Bitbucket
- GitHub Desktop and GitHub

Set up a repository

A *repository* is where you keep your work. You'll need a *local repository* where you edit and save files on your computer, and a *remote repository* online that lets people collaborate on the same project. A straightforward way to create both is to set up a repository with an online host and then *clone* it (create a local copy). Your collaborators can also clone the repository to their own computers, so everyone can keep in sync by pushing and pulling changes.

Bitbucket and Sourcetree

1. Sign up with Bitbucket and log on.
2. Click the new repository button (the plus sign):

3. Type a repository name, make sure it's set to be a public repository, and click **Create repository**.
4. Choose or create a directory on your computer where you would like to keep your local copy of the project.
5. Click **Clone in Sourcetree**.

6. Choose a folder on your computer for the local copy of the repository and click **Clone**.

GitHub and GitHub Desktop

1. Sign up with GitHub and log on.
2. Click the plus sign and select **New repository**:

3. Type a repository name, make sure it's set to be a public repository, and click **Create repository**.

4. Click **Set up in Desktop** to open the repository in GitHub Desktop:

5. Choose a folder on your computer for the local copy of the repository and click **Clone**.

It might not look like much has happened, but you now have:

- Git running on your computer
- A repository at an online Git host
- A local copy of the repository on your computer

Git basics

This page describes the workflows and commands you'll use in the recipes, and provides a few hints to get you out of trouble.

HINT: You don't have to read this page all the way through. Just refer to the parts you need.

Workflows

There are many possible Git workflows, but only two in this guide:

- **Git Centralized Workflow:** all work is done in a single branch
- **GitHub Flow:** different pieces of work are done in different branches

Centralized workflow

In the centralized workflow, everyone works on a single branch (usually called `master`). Changes are committed to the local repository on each contributor's own computer. From time to time, each user pushes changes to a remote Git repository.

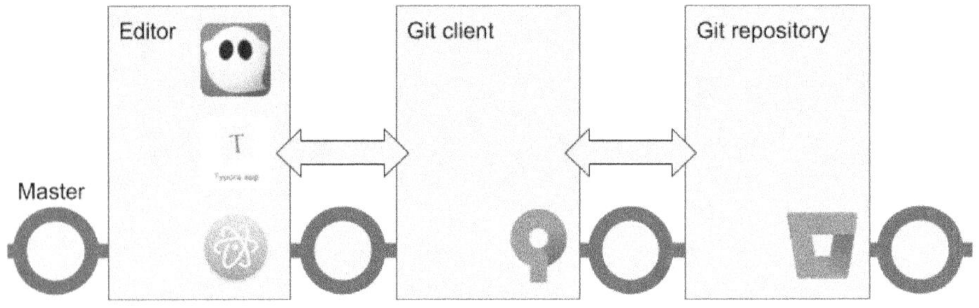

Here are the operations a contributor performs when working in the centralized workflow.

1. Pull	Fetch the latest changes from the remote repository to the local repository on your computer
2. Work	Edit your content in your favorite Markdown editor

<table>
<tr><td>3. Stage and commit</td><td>From time to time, in your Git client, type a short sentence about what you've done and save the changes to Git</td></tr>
<tr><td>4. Push</td><td>When your work is final, push it up to the remote repository</td></tr>
</table>

In the event that two people create conflicting changes, they can be manually resolved and then merged.

Although this workflow is called "centralized," it doesn't really resemble the old centralized source control model. The central remote repository is not a single source of truth, because every contributor has their own copy of the entire repository.

The following recipes use the centralized workflow:

- "Edit a Git wiki" on page 54
- "Collaborate using centralized Git workflow" on page 60

GitHub flow

In the GitHub flow, you start a new branch based on `master` whenever you start a group of related tasks. How you organize those tasks, and how you decide which ones belong in a branch together, is up to you.

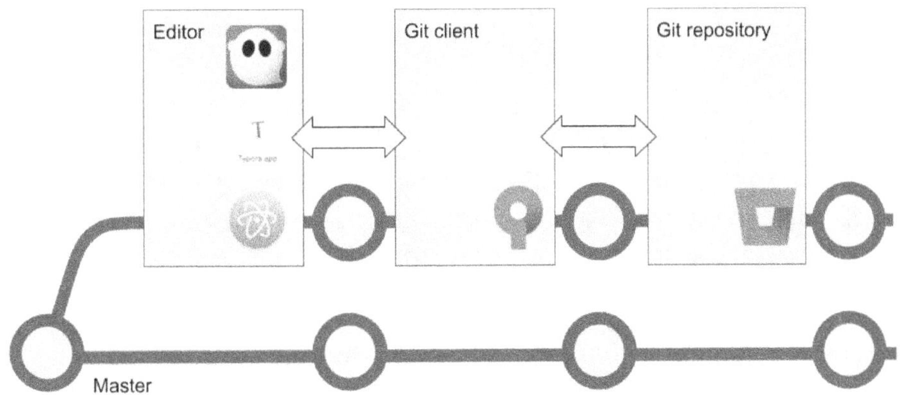

Just like in the centralized workflow, you commit changes frequently to your own local repository. When you push to the remote repo, you create a copy of your branch there so that others can review your changes before they are merged back into `master`.

Here's how your day looks in the GitHub flow.

1. Pull	Make sure you're on the master branch and sync the latest changes from the remote repository.
2. Create a branch	Create ("check out") a branch for working on the current part of the content.
3. Work	Edit your content in your favorite Markdown editor.
4. Stage and commit	From time to time, in your Git client, type a short sentence about what you've done and save the changes to Git.
5. Push	From time to time, sync your branch up to the remote repository.
6. Create a pull request	When your work is ready for review, create a pull request and add reviewers. If there's more work to do before final approval, you can edit your content, stage and commit, and push to the existing pull request.
7. Merge	When your work is approved, merge your branch into master on the remote repository.

Merge conflicts in your working branches are less likely, because you own your branches and other people don't necessarily work in them with you. Conflicts are more likely to happen between your working branch and the master branch on the remote repo. Before you push your branch to the remote repo, you can pull from master again and merge any conflicts locally.

HINT: After you've pushed, approved, and merged your work, you can delete your working branch or keep it around for further work. When you start work on a different part of the project, remember to switch to master and pull again before creating a new branch.

The following recipe uses the GitHub flow:

- "Manage docs with GitHub Flow" on page 62

How to Git

These are the commands that make up the steps in the Git workflows.

Pull

The Git pull command fetches and downloads content from your remote repository, automatically merges the changes with your local repository, and updates everything so that your repository matches the latest version of everything on the remote. It's a good idea to pull after making sure you're on the right branch and before starting to work on the content.

Sourcetree

1. Make sure you're on the right branch in the correct repository:
   - The bold text under **Branches** tells you the branch
   - The tab at the top of the screen tells you the repository
2. Select **Repository > Pull** or click the **Pull** button.

Pull

GitHub Desktop

In GitHub Desktop, you can *fetch* and *pull* separately. Fetch gets the latest updates from origin but doesn't update your local working copy with the changes. After you click **Fetch origin**, the button changes to **Pull Origin**.

1. Make sure you're on the right branch in the correct repository:
   - The bold text under **Current branch** tells you the branch
   - The bold text under **Current repository** tells you the repository
2. Select **Repository > Pull** or:

a.   Click the **Fetch origin** button.

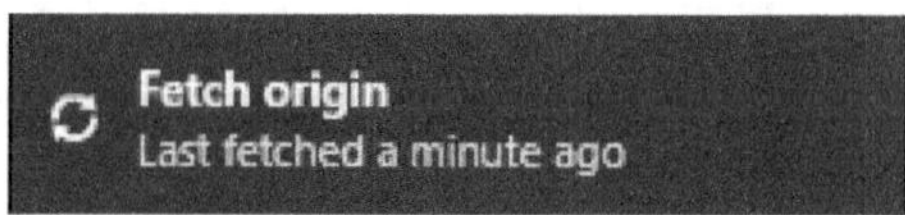

b.   Click the **Pull origin** button.

Linux command line

1.   Make sure you're on the right branch in the correct repository:
```
$ git branch
* master
$ git remote -v
origin  https://github.com/pconrad-fb/markdown.git
(fetch)
origin  https://github.com/pconrad-fb/markdown.git
(push)
```

2.   Type the `git pull` command:
```
$ git pull
```

Stage and commit

Git knows when you make changes to your files. When you want to save those changes to Git, you must do two things:

- *stage* them, which tells Git which changes you intend to keep
- *commit* them, which saves the changes.

Sourcetree

In Sourcetree, you stage and commit your files in two operations.

1.   Make sure you're on the right branch in the correct repository.
2.   Look for the files you changed in the Unstaged files pane. Select the files you want to stage—in most cases, you can just click **Stage All.**

3. Make sure you see the right files in the Staged files pane.

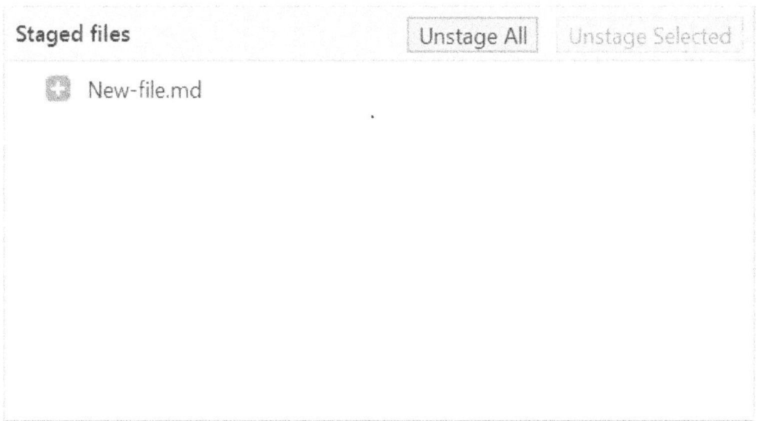

4. Type a short commit message and click **Commit**.

GitHub Desktop

In GitHub Desktop, you can stage and commit your files in one step.

1. Make sure you're on the right branch in the correct repository.

2. Look for the files you changed in the Changes tab. Unselect any files you don't want to change—most of the time, you can leave all the checkboxes checked.

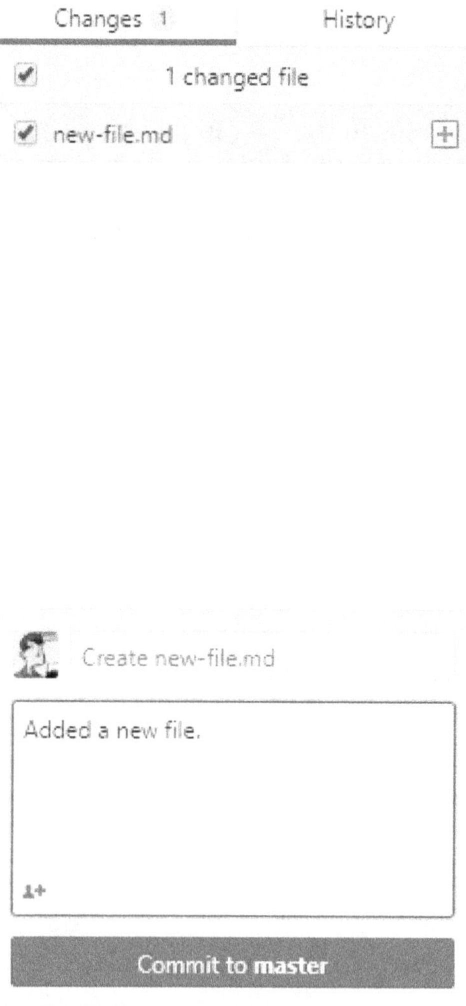

3. Type a short commit message.

4. Make sure the **Commit** button refers to the correct branch
    ("Commit to master," for example).

5. Click **Commit to [branch]**.

Linux command line

1. Make sure you're on the right branch in the correct repository.

2. Use `git status` to see what changes are not yet staged.

3. Stage any changes you plan to commit. In many cases, you can
    stage all the changes at once like this:

    ```
    $ git add *
    ```

4. Commit the changes, adding a descriptive message:

    ```
    $ git commit -m "Type your descriptive message here."
    ```

    HINT: If you are changing files but not adding or deleting any files,
    you can often stage and commit all in one line with `commit -am`
    like so:

    ```
    $ git commit -am "Type your descriptive message
    here."
    ```

Push

Sourcetree

*   Make sure you're on the right branch in the correct repository.
*   Select **Repository > Push** or click the **Push** button.

Push

GitHub Desktop

1. Make sure you're on the right branch in the correct repository.
2. Select Repository > Push or click the Push origin button.

Linux command line

1. Make sure you're on the right branch in the correct repository.
2. Push, specifying the remote (usually `origin`) and the branch. For the recipes where you are working on the master branch, the command looks like this:

```
$ git push origin master
```

3. Of course, since git knows what branch you're on and where your remote is, you can sometimes just type `git push`.

Create a branch

Sourcetree

1. Pull from master.
2. Click the **Branch** button:

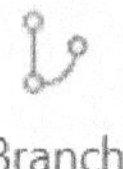

3. Type a descriptive name and click **Create Branch**.

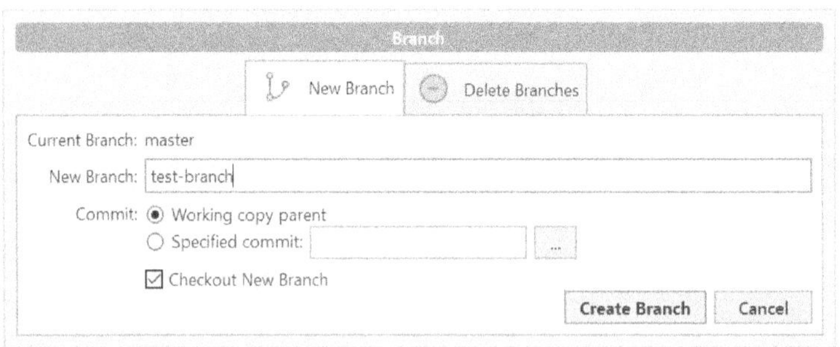

4. Look under **Branches** to see that you're on the new branch.

GitHub Desktop

1. **Pull** from master.
2. Click the **Current branch** tab and click **New branch**:

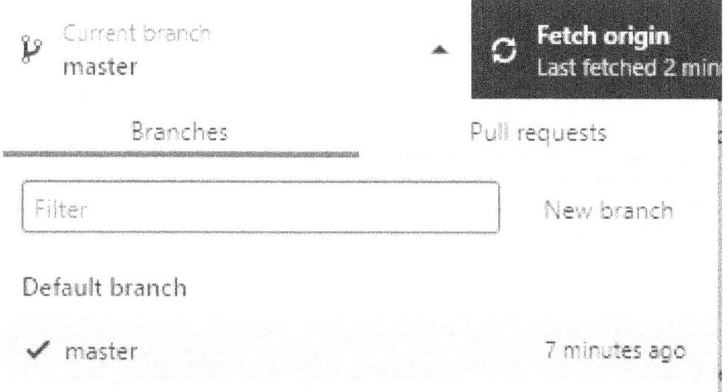

3. Type a descriptive name and click **Create branch**:

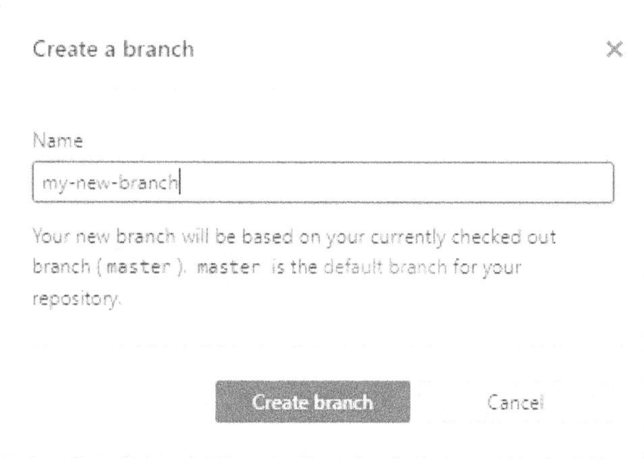

4. Click **Publish branch**:

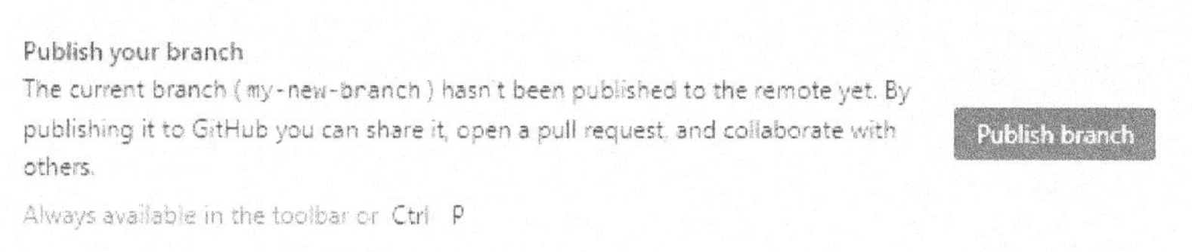

5. Look under **Branches** to see that you're on the new branch.

Linux command line

1. Pull from master to make sure you have the latest changes:

```
$ git checkout master
Already on 'master'
Your branch is up to date with 'origin/master'.
$ git pull
Already up to date.
```

2. Create a new branch and switch to it with git checkout -b. Example:

```
$ git checkout -b test-branch
Switched to a new branch 'test-branch'
```

HINT: You can switch to any existing branch by typing git checkout <branch-name> without the -b. Example:
```
$ git checkout test-branch
Switched to branch 'test-branch'
```

NOTE: You can't switch branches with uncommitted changes. You have to commit or stash before switching to a new branch.

Create a pull request

Bitbucket and Sourcetree

1. Click **Repository > Create pull request**.
2. In the dialog that appears, click **Create Pull Request On Web**:

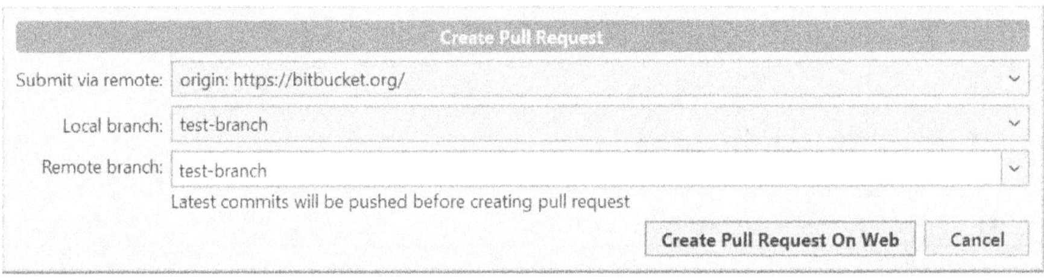

3. Type a description, add reviewers, and click **Create pull request**:

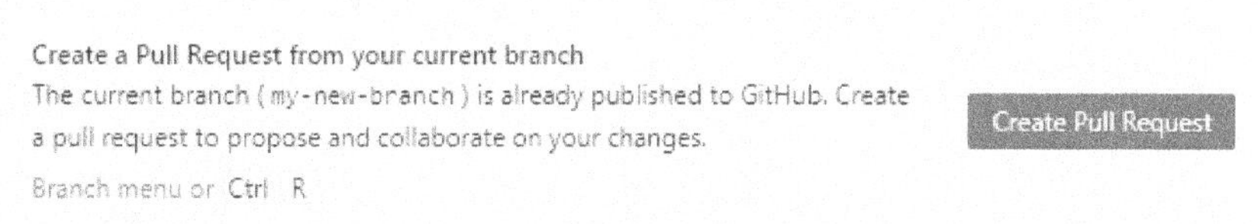

GitHub and GitHub Desktop

1. When you push, the banner with the Push button changes to read "Create a pull request from your current branch." Click **Create Pull Request**:

2. The browser opens a page with a form for creating a pull request:

Open a pull request

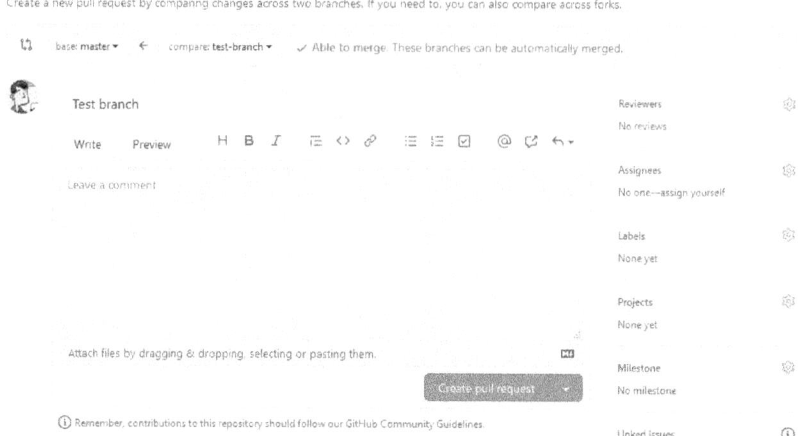

3. Click the gear next to **Reviewers** to add reviewers:

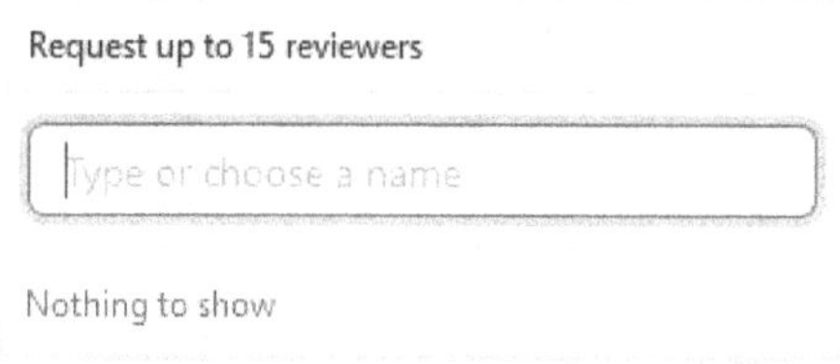

4. Click **Create pull request**.

1. Take a look at the output from the push command:

```
$ git push origin test-branch
Enumerating objects: 14, done.
Counting objects: 100% (14/14), done.
Delta compression using up to 4 threads
Compressing objects: 100% (10/10), done.
Writing objects: 100% (10/10), 4.39 KiB | 1.10 MiB/s,
done.
Total 10 (delta 2), reused 0 (delta 0)
remote: Resolving deltas: 100% (2/2), completed with 1
local object.  remote:
remote: Create a pull request for 'test-branch' on
GitHub by visiting:  remote:
https://github.com/pconrad/markdown/pull/new/testbranch
remote:
To https://github.com/pconrad-fb/markdown.git
 * [new branch]      test-branch -> test-branch
```

2. Copy the URL from the line after `Create a pull request` into a browser.
3. Follow the instructions on screen. If you get stuck, you can see some hints in the instructions for Bitbucket or GitHub.

Approve and merge

Merge your branch online in the web interface of your Git host.

Bitbucket

1. When your pull request is sufficiently approved, click **Merge**:

1. When your pull request is sufficiently approved, click **Merge**:

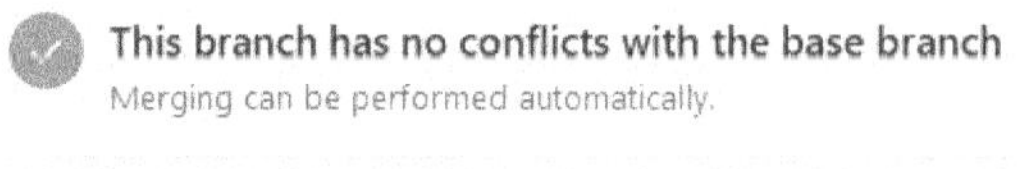

Getting out of trouble

If you get out into the woods with Git, there's usually a way to get back—but for this kind of magic, you have to go to the command line.

Working in the wrong branch

You've edited a file in the wrong branch. What you'd like to be able to do is undo those changes, switch branches, then re-do them. Actually, it would be even better to lift those changes off of the wrong branch, laying them gently on top of the branch you meant to be in. Fortunately, Git provides a command called `stash` that does exactly that.

1. Make sure you're in the right directory.
2. Use `git status` to check what branch you're on and what changes Git knows about.
3. Make sure you're in the branch where you were erroneously working. For example:

   ```
   $ git checkout the-wrong-branch
     Switched to branch 'the-wrong-branch'
   ```

4. Stash your uncommitted changes:

   ```
   $ git stash
   ```

5. Switch to the branch you wish you had been working in:

   ```
   $ git checkout -b the-wrong-branch
   Switched to branch 'the-wrong-branch'
   ```

6. Use `stash` to apply the changes there:

   ```
   $ git stash apply
   ```

Editing the wrong file

You opened a file to look at it, but then your cat walked across the keyboard. You're not sure what was added or deleted. You just want to go back to the way things were at the last commit. For this, use checkout—it's not just for switching branches, but also for fixing changes to files.

1. Make sure you're in the right directory.
2. Use `git status` to check what branch you're on and what changes Git knows about.
3. If necessary, switch to the correct branch. For example:

```
$ git checkout the-branch
Switched to branch 'the-branch'
```

4. Use `git status` to see what files were accidentally modified. For example:

```
$ git status
On branch master
Changes not staged for commit:
  (use "git add <file>..." to update what will be
committed)
  (use "git checkout -- <file>..." to discard changes
in working directory)

        modified:   dont-change-this.md
```

5. Use `git checkout -- <file>` to undo the changes. For example:

```
git checkout -- dont-change-this.md
```

HINT: The output of the `git status` command tells you how to use `git checkout` this way.

Staged too soon

You edited the right file the right way, but then you added it to the staging area too hastily. You don't want to undo your changes to the file, but you would like to remove it from the next commit. This is one of the uses of `reset`. You can also use `reset` to do more drastic rollbacks—you can undo entire commits if needed.

1. Make sure you're in the right directory.
2. Use `git status` to check what branch you're on and what changes Git knows about.

3.   If necessary, switch to the correct branch. For example:

```
$ git checkout the-branch
Switched to branch 'the-branch'
```

4.   Use `git status` to see what files were accidentally modified. For example:

```
$ git status
On branch master
Changes to be committed:
  (use "git reset HEAD <file>..." to unstage)

    renamed:    README.md -> README
    modified:   dont-commit-this.md
```

5.   Use `git reset` to remove the file from the next commit. For example:

```
git reset HEAD dont-commit-this.md
```

HINT: After you've pushed, the output of the `git status` command tells you how to use `reset` to unstage changes.

Merge conflicts

When two changes happen at the same place in the same file, can't automatically merge. You need to edit the file and decide which of the two changes to keep. When you open the file, the merge conflict looks like this:

```
<<<<<<< HEAD
Some content that was changed
=======
Other content that was also changed
>>>>>>> 9af9d3b
```

HEAD is a pointer to the most recent commit in the branch you're on. The other label can be another branch name or a number representing another commit.

Decide which version of the content you want to keep and then delete the merge conflict markers (<<<<<<<, =======, >>>>>>>). After you've resolved all the changes in that way, just commit again.

For more help, check out Dangit, Git!?! (see "Links" on page 125).

Publishing tools

There are many tools for publishing Markdown or converting it for use in other doc tools. We'll focus on the Git wiki, the static site generators Hugo and MkDocs, and Pandoc. We'll also touch on tools for creating presentations.

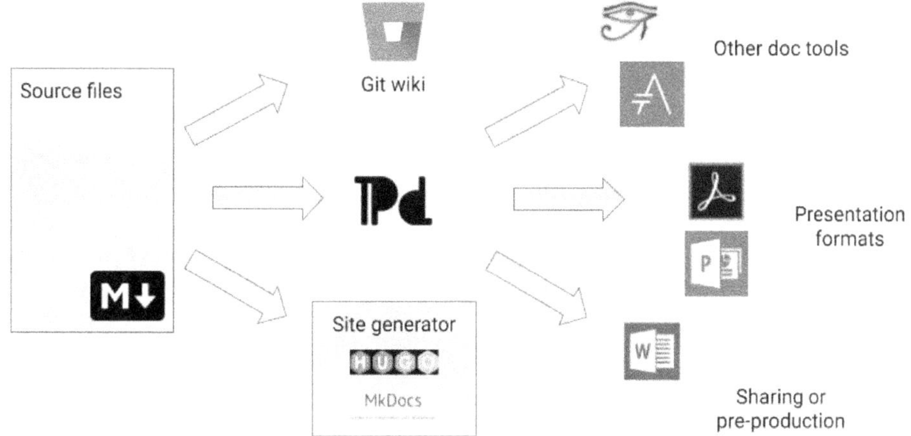

Diagram of publishing tools

Git wiki

A Git wiki is a special additional repository attached to your Git code repository. You create and clone a git wiki separately from your main repository.

Git wiki structure

A Git wiki uses folders to organize files. The path to a file is used to create the URL where the content is displayed.

A simple directory structure might look like this:

```
Home.md
stuff/
    something.md
```

In that case, the URL to the content in `something.md` is:
/wiki/stuff/something

Hugo

Hugo is an open-source static site generator that includes templates and provides exensibility in the form of *shortcodes,* which provide additional formatting. You can even create your own shortcodes.

MkDocs

MkDocs is a static site generator that turns directories of Markdown files into a searchable, presentable documentation website. Customizable themes, many of them provided by the community, provide Markdown extensions for reusing content and for formatting such as tabs and admonitions.

HINT: According to its inventor, Tom Christie, "MkDocs" is spoken using "the 'Scottish pronunciation'—as in McDocs, McDonald, McGregor, etc."

Pandoc

Pandoc is a tool that can convert between Markdown and a number of formats. You can use Pandoc to create Word and Powerpoint documents, PDFs, HTML, and several kinds of presentations. For longer documents, can concatenate Markdown files together.

Pandoc includes formatting tricks that let you do things like creating columns or scaling images, and you can use stylesheets from existing documents to give your content a specific look and feel.

You can also convert from various formats to Markdown, including doing things like grabbing a web page as a Markdown file. You can even try it online.

FTP

When you create a website with Hugo or MkDocs, you'll use file transfer protocol (FTP) to upload the files to the web. You can do this from the command line, but it's much easier to choose an application that gives a nice UI and lets you save bookmarks.

Here are a few:

- **FileZilla** - a free, open source FTP tool for macOS and Windows
- **gFTP** - the default Linux option
- **Transmit** - a commercial file transfer app for macOS

Presentation tools

Here are two tools that you can use for in-browser presentations: DZSlides and Remark. You can also use Pandoc to create PowerPoint presentations.

DZSlides

DZSlides is a single page, HTML-based slide presentation template. Pandoc can generate a DZSlides presentation from a Markdown file.

Remark

Remark is an in-browser presentation tool made from Javascript, HTML, CSS, and, of course, Markdown. The slideshow lives in a <textarea> tag where you can add and edit Markdown directly.

Other tools

If you are converting Markdown to a format such as Word, PDF, or ePub, it can be useful to have editing tools to help you fix any problems in the final result:

- **Acrobat** - the original PDF reader
- **LibreOffice** - an open-source office suite
- **Microsoft Office** - an office suite that includes Word and PowerPoint
- **Sigil** - a multi-platform ePub editor

Take notes

Markdown is a great tool for taking notes quickly, because you can accomplish all the basic formatting without taking your hands off the keyboard. A note-taking app like Joplin or a Markdown editor like Typora can help you organize your notes. You can add Cloud storage like Dropbox to share your notes among devices.

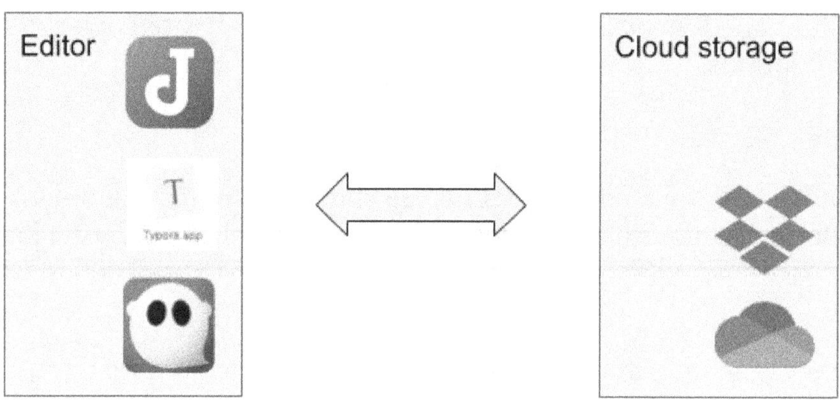

This recipe describes two tools for taking notes:

- Joplin
- Typora

Ingredients

- Markdown editor
- Cloud storage

Joplin

Joplin is designed specifically for taking notes, and shares some features with applications like Evernote. You can store your notes as local files on your computer, or sync them to the cloud with a service like Dropbox or OneDrive. You can even encrypt your notes end-to-end for privacy.

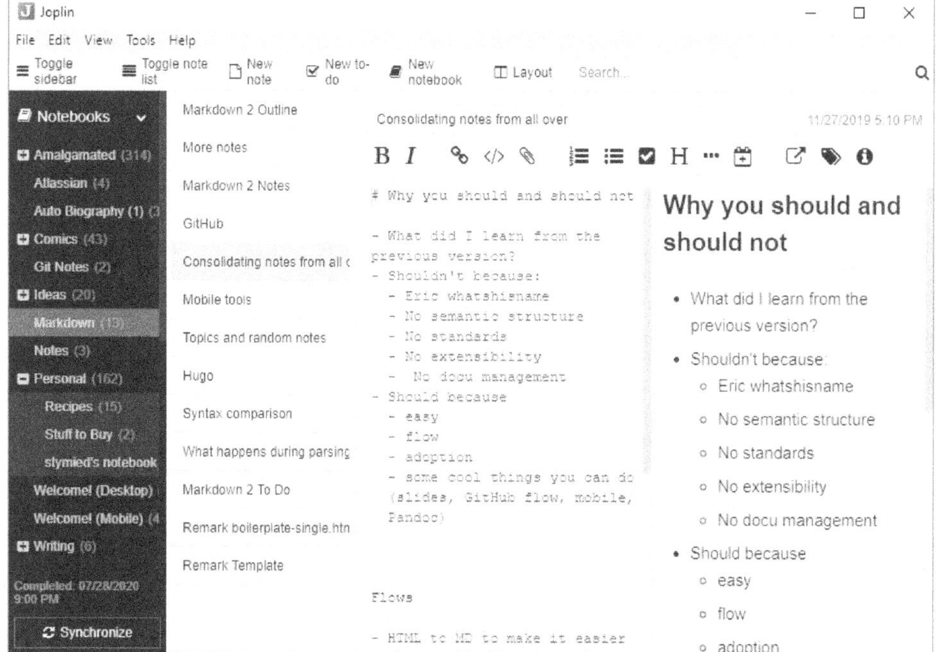

Setting up Joplin is fairly straightforward. In the **Preferences** screen, there is a place to choose your storage: local filesystem, DropBox, and so on. If you want to sync Joplin across devices, configure all your Joplin instances to use the same cloud storage location.

Getting your old notes from Evernote

One of the great features of Joplin is that you can import notes from Evernote. The caveat is that the imported Markdown files will not have sensible filenames—but this is still better than manually copying and pasting each note.

To export each notebook from Evernote:

1. In Evernote, right click a notebook in the left nav and select **Export notes**.

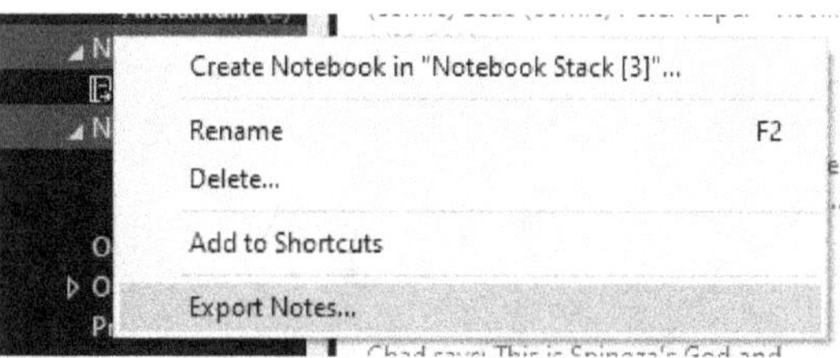

2. Export the notebook as an ENEX file.

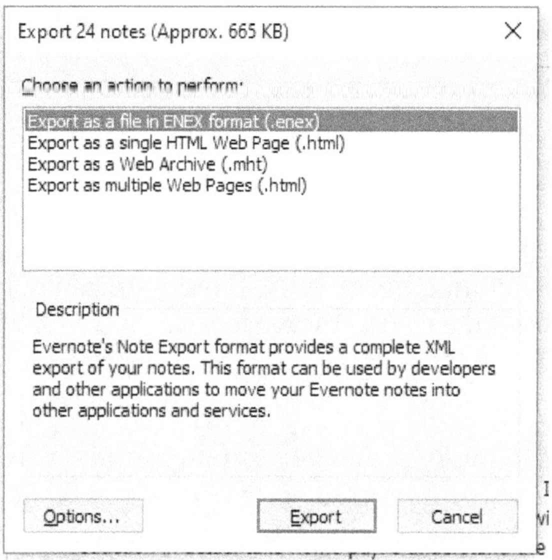

3.   In Joplin, go to **File > Import** and import the notebook as Markdown.

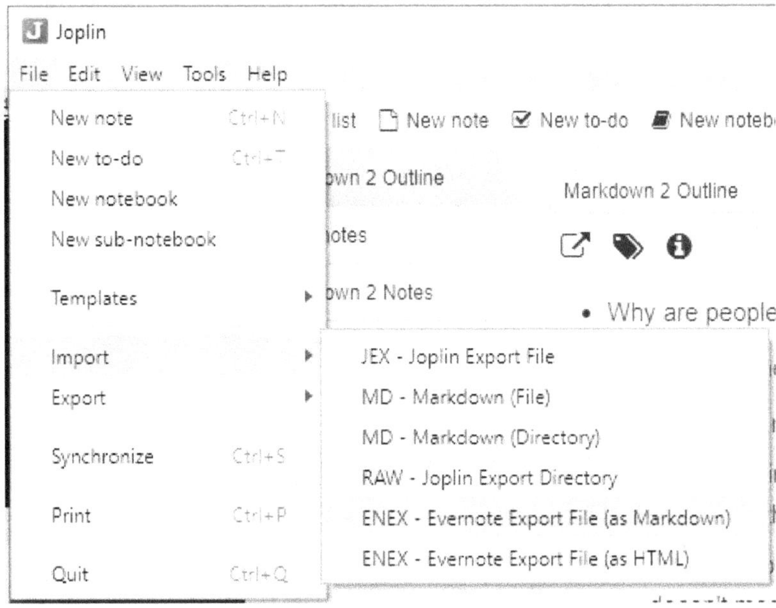

4. If you wish, you can then export the notebook as Markdown from Joplin into the folder where you have decided to store your notes.

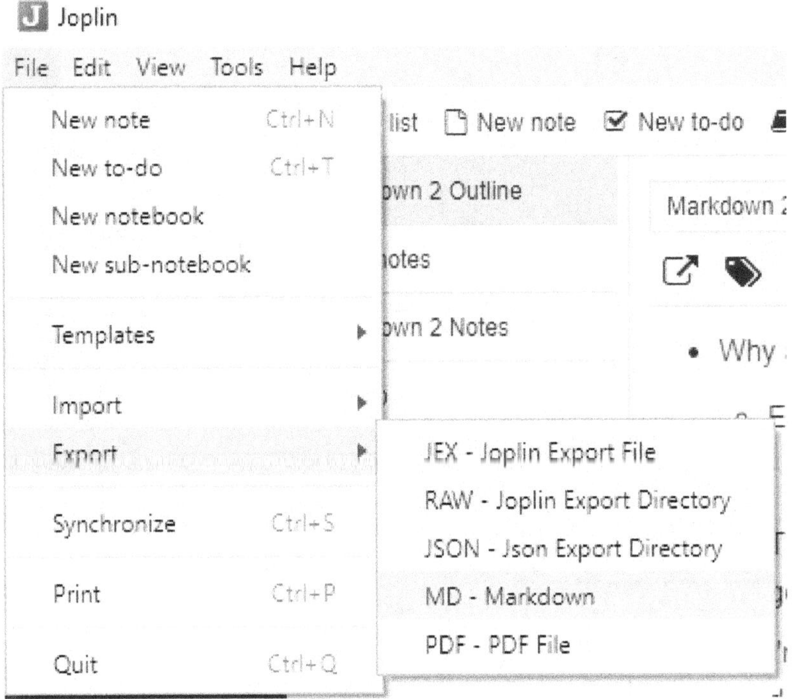

Typora

As an alternative to Joplin, you can use another editor such as Typora. Both Joplin and Typora provide a navigation tree to make it easy to organize and manage "notes" (which are just Markdown files). The advantage of Joplin is that it is a dedicated note-taking app. The advantage of Typora is that it is a Markdown editor, which means you get a lot more tools for integrating into a content management and publishing toolchain. If you plan to do more than just note-taking, consider Typora or another Markdown editor like Ghostwriter. Actually, there's nothing stopping you from using all three!

Installing and using Typora is pretty straightforward. You can store files in multiple folders, which makes it easy to set up a note-taking folder, a drafts folder, a documents folder, and so on. Any of these folders could by synced by Dropbox or another service.

HINT: You can use Joplin to get your old notes from Evernote, then use Typora to manage and edit them.

Setting up Typora to take notes

To fine-tune Typora as a note-taking application, set a few preferences:

1.   Go to **File > Preferences**.
2.   Click the **General** tab.

3.   For *On Launch*, select **Restore last closed folders**. When you set up a folder to contain your notes, Typora will open it for you

automatically. Of course, you can also open other files and folders.

4. Check the **Auto Save** checkbox and make sure **Save without asking...** is checked. You won't have to think about saving notes; they'll just always be saved.

5. Click the **Image** tab.

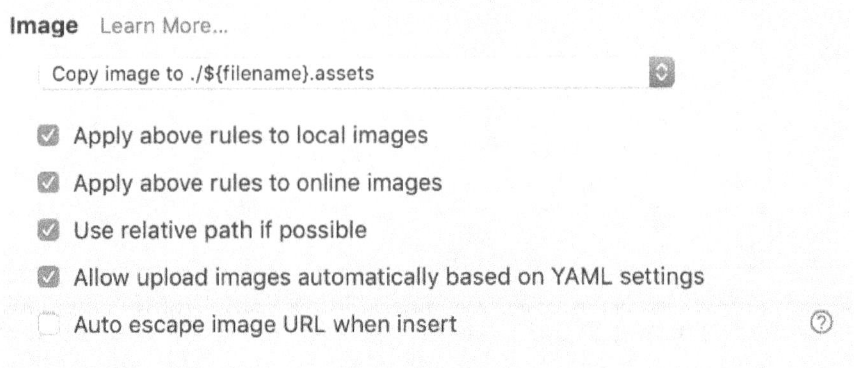

6. Select **Copy image to ./${filename}.assets**. Typora will make a folder for each
document's images. This makes it easy to take the images along if you convert the document to a different format or send it to another location.

7. Check all the boxes except for the auto escape one. This makes sure that local files and online images also get added to the `.assets` folder. By the way, Typora saves copies of pasted images, too!

8.   Click the **Markdown** tab.

9.   Check the **Highlight** box so that you can highlight things in your
     notes.

Edit a Git wiki

A Git repository comes with a wiki, where people can read and collaboratively edit documentation. You can create a wiki to document projects or code stored in the repository, or you can just use a repository for its wiki capability.

NOTE: A Git wiki is a second repository attached to your repository. You clone, pull, and push to the main repository and the wiki separately.

A Git wiki uses Git wiki structure and it's one way to develop content for publishing in MkDocs or Hugo.

HINT: If you use a Git wiki to develop content for Hugo, remember to add YAML frontmatter at the beginning of each file.

Ingredients

- Markdown editor
- Git

Set up a wiki on your hosted repository

The easiest way to set up the wiki is by logging onto your Git host and adding it there.

Bitbucket and Sourcetree

1. In a browser, log on to Bitbucket.

2. Under "Repository settings" look for "Features" and click **Wiki**.

3.   Select **Public wiki** and save.

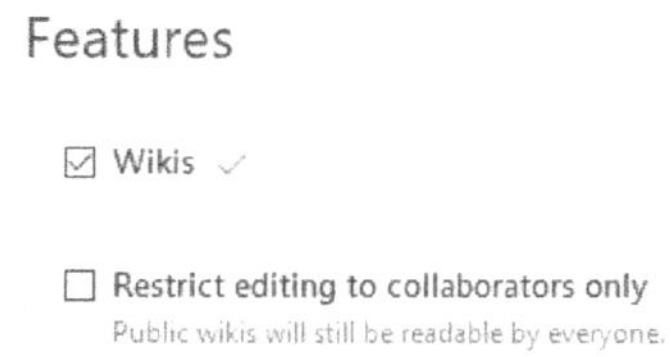

GitHub and GitHub Desktop

The GitHub documentation on wikis is helpful (see "Links" on page 125). Here are the basic steps to set up a wiki on GitHub:

1.   In a browser, log on to GitHub.
2.   Click the **Settings** button:

> ⚙ Settings

3.   Scroll down to "Features" and select **Wikis**:

Features

☑ Wikis ✓

☐ Restrict editing to collaborators only
  Public wikis will still be readable by everyone.

Edit content on the host

If you just want to add a few pages to the wiki online, there's no more setup to do! Just go to your repository, click **Wiki**, and you'll see buttons for creating and editing pages.

HINT: To add a page in a new folder, make the folder part of the new filename. For example: `morestuff/newpage.md` adds `newpage.md` in a folder called `morestuff`.

Clone the wiki to a local repository

There are advantages to working with wiki files locally, on your own computer:

- It's much easier to add folders and move files around
- You can work on it even when you're offline
- You can use whatever Markdown editor you want
- Others can collaborate with you

To work on the wiki locally, clone the wiki to a local repository:

Bitbucket and Sourcetree

1. Go to your online repository and click **Wiki**.

2. Click **Clone wiki** then **Clone in Sourcetree**.

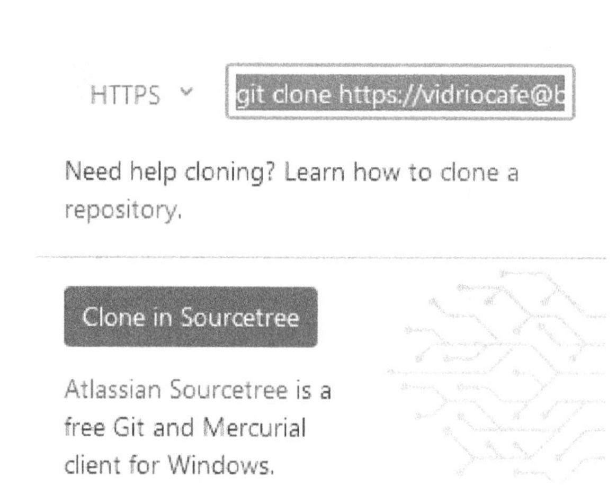

3. Make sure the local path shows the directory where you want to clone the repository, and click **Clone**.

GitHub and GitHub Desktop

1. Go to your online repository and click the **Wiki** button:

    Wiki

2. Copy the **Clone this wiki locally** URL. 1. In GitHub Desktop, click **File > Clone repository**.

3. Paste the URL, make sure the local path shows the directory where you want to clone the repository, and click **Clone**.

Linux command line

1. Go to your online repository and click **Wiki**.

2. Copy the URL (or command and URL) to clone the wiki repository.

3. On the command line, navigate to the directory where you want to clone the repository.

4. Use `git clone` and the URL to clone the repository. Example:

```
git clone
https://my_name@bitbucket.org/my_name/markdown-
stuff.git/wiki
```

Work with the content locally

On your computer, go to the directory where you cloned the wiki. There should be a directory called `wiki` containing a file called `Home.md` containing the Markdown source for the welcome page the wiki displayed when you created it online.

You can now work with the wiki using the Git centralized workflow or the GitHub flow, using the familiar cycle of pull, edit, commit, push.

Tutorial

Here's a quick tutorial that shows how to organize pages in the wiki.

Try creating some content

Try making the following changes:

- Add a folder called `stuff`.
- Using your favorite Markdown editor, make a file called `something.md` inside `stuff`, with the following contents:

```
# Something

Yes, there's *something* here! Now go [home](../Home).
```

You should now have a directory structure that looks like this:

```
Home.md
stuff/
    something.md
```

Take a look

After you commit and push the changes, take a look in your online wiki:

1. Go to your online repository and click **Wiki**.
2. View the page tree of the wiki. For example:
    - In Bitbucket, click the name of the wiki.
    - In GitHub, click **Pages**.

3. Navigate to the page you created.

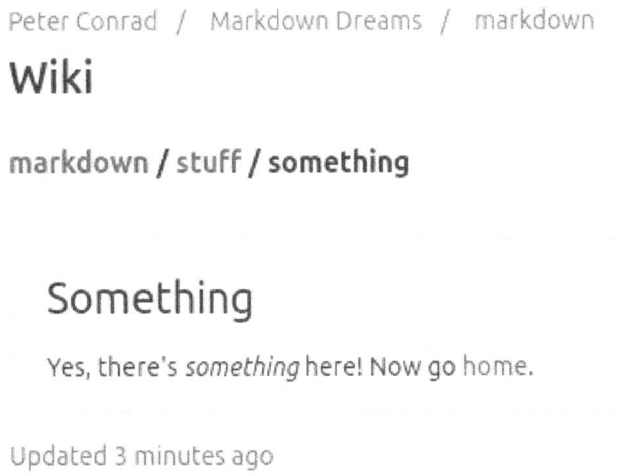
Peter Conrad / Markdown Dreams / markdown
Wiki
markdown / stuff / something
Something
Yes, there's *something* here! Now go home.
Updated 3 minutes ago

4. Try the home link.

Collaborate using centralized Git workflow

You can use Git to help a team collaborate on informal or internal documents in a very simple way. If you use a graphical Git client and a WYSIWYG Markdown editor, the workflow is easy for people who like things simple. At the same time, Markdown in Git is powerful enough for engineers and integrates with their tools.

The centralized workflow can be an effective way for content creators, managers, and engineers to collaborate on non-production content such as specifications, planning documents, newsletters, internal documentation, and the like.

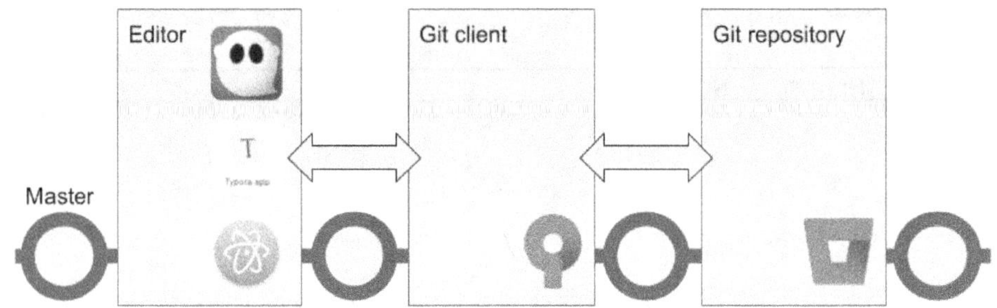

In this workflow, everyone works on the same branch. This makes things easy for simple collaboration.

NOTE: If you're publishing a large website or documentation set in a production environment with with a substantial number of collaborators, you should consider using GitHub Flow instead.

Ingredients

- Markdown editor
- Git
- Publishing tools (optional)

HINT: Plan ahead based on the publishing tool you want to use. If you're planning to use a wiki, MkDocs, or Hugo, organize your docs in Git wiki structure and add YAML frontmatter from the start. If you're creating large documents with Pandoc, think about whether you need to work on content in pieces and then use Pandoc to assemble everything.

Working with content

This recipe uses the centralized Git workflow. Pick an editor, then make sure you have Git set up and try each step below. The steps work together like a heartbeat that keeps content safe and synchronized for all collaborators.

1. Pull	Fetch the latest changes from the remote repository to the local repository on your computer
2. Work	Edit your content in your favorite Markdown editor
3. Stage and commit	From time to time, in your Git client, type a short sentence about what you've done and save the changes to Git
4. Push	When your work is final, push it up to the remote repository

HINT: Remember not to publish content into a Git repository. The repo is only for storing your Markdown and other source files.

Manage docs with GitHub Flow

Once your team or project reaches a certain size, branching is a good way to keep people from accidentally interfering with each other's work. It's also a great way to stage and test code or content before migrating to production. There are many branching strategies, some of them quite complicated. The one I like, and that I have used for documentation in the past, is called GitHub Flow. It's simple but effective. The **Pull-Work-Commit-Push** steps happen within a working branch.

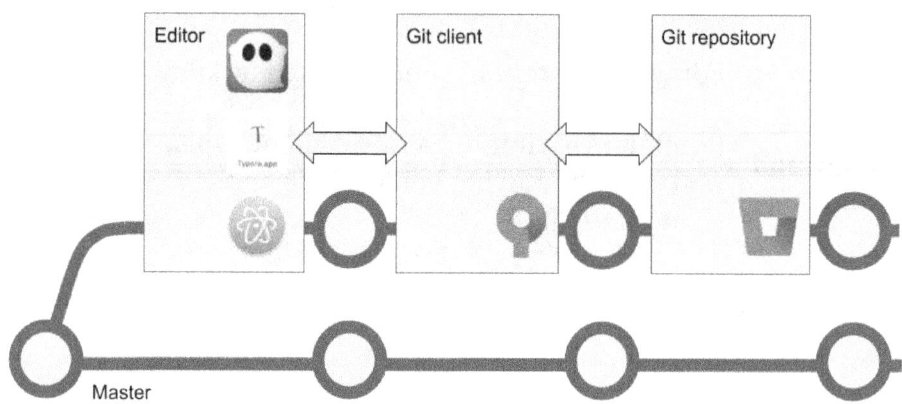

Ingredients

- Markdown editor
- Git
- Publishing tools

HINT: Plan ahead based on the publishing tool you want to use. If you're planning to use a wiki, MkDocs, or Hugo, organize your docs in Git wiki structure and add YAML frontmatter from the start. If you're creating large documents with Pandoc, think about whether you need to work on content in pieces and then use Pandoc to assemble everything.

Working with content

Pick an editor, then make sure you have Git set up and try each step below. The steps work together like a heartbeat that keeps content safe and synchronized for all collaborators.

1. Pull

Make sure you're on the master branch and sync the latest changes from the remote repository.

2. Create a branch

Create ("check out") a branch for working on the current part of the content.

3. Work

Edit your content in your favorite Markdown editor.

4. Stage and commit

From time to time, in your Git client, type a short sentence about what you've done and save the changes to Git.

5. Push

From time to time, sync your branch up to the remote repository.

6. Create a pull request

When your work is ready for review, create a pull request and add reviewers. If there's more work to do before final approval, you can edit your content, stage and commit, an push to the existing pull request.

7. Merge

When your work is approved, merge your branch into master on the remote repository

HINT: After you're done with that part of the project, you can delete your working branch or keep it around for further work. Before starting work on a different part of the project, remember to switch to master and pull again.

Remember not to publish content into a Git repository. The repo is only for storing your Markdown and other source files.

Publish a website with Hugo

Hugo is a very powerful open-source static site generator that includes tools for organizing content, adding extensions, and even creating dynamic logic. There is way too much to document here, so the focus of this recipe will be getting started and a few basics.

To install Hugo, use your operating system's package manager:

- Linux: apt-get or yum
- macOS: Homebrew
- Windows: Chocolatey

Ingredients

- Markdown editor
- Hugo
- Git (optional)

HINT: Hugo works best with Markdown files that are organized in Git wiki structure. You can even use Git wiki to develop the content, so long as you add YAML frontmatter as you go.

This recipe goes well with:

- Centralized Git workflow
- GitHub flow

Setting up your site

Once Hugo is installed, you can create a new site by typing `hugo new site my-project`, which provides some instructions when it runs:

```
$ hugo new site my-project
Congratulations! Your new Hugo site is created in /home/pco
nrad/git/my-project.

Just a few more steps and you're ready to go:

1. Download a theme into the same-named folder.
   Choose a theme from https://themes.gohugo.io/ or
   create your own with the "hugo new theme <THEMENAME>"

   command.
2. Perhaps you want to add some content. You can add single
files
   with "hugo new <SECTIONNAME>/<FILENAME>.<FORMAT>".
3. Start the built-in live server via "hugo server".

Visit https://gohugo.io/ for quickstart guide and full docu
mentation.
```

HINT: For source control and collaboration, create the project in a Git repo.

Adding a theme

To add a theme, you use the `git submodule add` command from within your site directory. Each theme in Hugo's official Complete List includes instructions for adding the submodule from the correct Git repository. Example:

```
$ git submodule add https://github.com/budparr/gohugo-theme
-ananke.git themes/ananke
Cloning into '/home/pconrad/git/my-project/themes/ananke'..
.
remote: Enumerating objects: 8, done.
remote: Counting objects: 100% (8/8), done.
remote: Compressing objects: 100% (8/8), done.
remote: Total 1839 (delta 2), reused 1 (delta 0), pack-reus
ed 1831
Receiving objects: 100% (1839/1839), 4.33 MiB | 1.26 MiB/s,
done.
Resolving deltas: 100% (1022/1022), done.
```

After you've installed the theme, add it to the configuration file `config.toml`. Example:

```
$ echo 'theme = "ananke"' >> config.toml
```

Edit the `config.toml` file to change other things about the site, such as the site title or the base URL.

Working with content

You can create a new page with `hugo new <path>`. For example, to create a new post in the `posts` directory, type:

```
hugo new posts/my-first-post.md
```

When it's created, all this page contains is YAML frontmatter:

```
---
title: "My First Post"
date: 2020-08-28T18:42:02-07:00
draft: true
---
```

You must add Markdown content before you can preview the page. A page in Hugo must contain both frontmatter and Markdown content. If either is missing, the page shows 404 page not found when you try to preview it.

Frontmatter can signal content status, including publish and expiry dates, and can contain variables. You can use the variables in templates and in content by creating your own Hugo shortcodes. Variables and shortcodes are outside the scope of this recipe, but the Hugo website has a lot of documentation.

If you are migrating content into Hugo from a Git wiki, MkDocs site, or some other source, you will need to add frontmatter to any pages that don't already have it.

Local preview

To preview your content, start the Hugo server:

```
$ hugo server -D
```

The -D option tells Hugo to include draft pages in the preview. If you omit this option, any page with draft:true in the frontmatter is ignored.

Here is a screenshot of a Markdown file with frontmatter, and the same content previewed in Hugo.

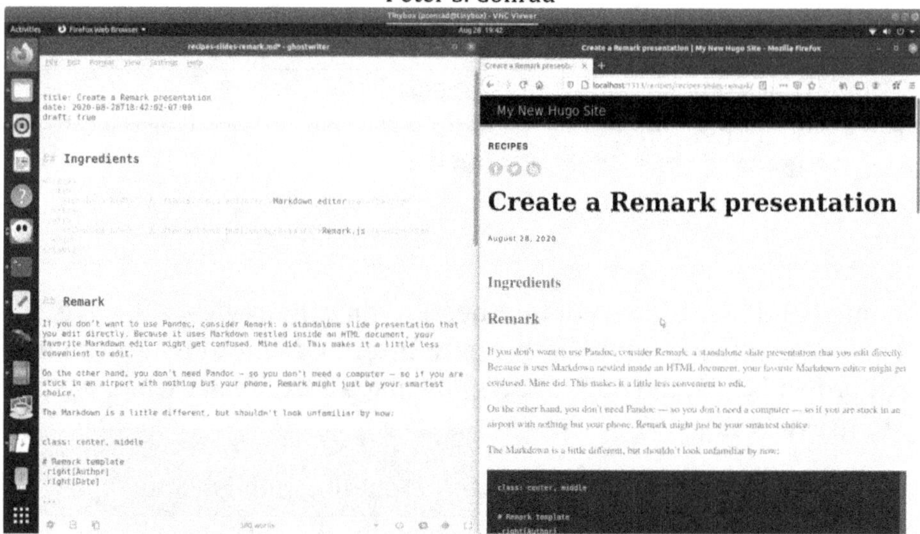

Hugo is a bit finicky about previewing and building content, and there are a few reasons why a page might not show up in the preview. A first troubleshooting step is to make sure the file contains both frontmatter and Markdown, and that it doesn't have a publish date in the future or expiry date in the past.

Images

Images in Hugo normally go in the `static` directory. Here, I've added a subdirectory called `images` and when I add the image in my Markdown editor it looks like this:

```
![An image](../../static/images/whatever.png)
```

That makes sense, since that is the correct relative path to the file. When the site is built for local preview, however, the result is this:

```
<img src="../../static/images/whatever.png" alt="An image">
```

Unfortunately, that won't work. The actual relative path to the image is: `../../images/whatever.png` instead.

In other words, when you add an image whose relative path is correct with regard to the Markdown file, you must remove `static/` from the path to make it work in the preview and the built site. If you are using an editor that lets you preview the images as you work, then you have to break all the images to get them to work in Hugo.

One solution might be to upload all your images to the web first, then use absolute paths—but this will make it more difficult to move the website or change the paths later.

Building and publishing

The `hugo` command builds the website in a directory called `public`. To publish the site, use FTP to transfer the contents of that directory to a folder on a webserver.

HINT: To prevent Git from tracking changes to the `public` directory, create a file called `.gitignore` at the top level directory of the Hugo project with the following contents:

```
public/
```

If you use `git add` to add your `.gitignore` file to change tracking, then it will apply to anyone who clones the repo—meaning that no one will add built HTML pages to Git.

Publish documentation with MkDocs

MkDocs is a static site generator designed for documentation. It's fairly easy to use, though it does require some comfort with the command line. Like some other tools, it uses the Git wiki structure—which means you can use Git wiki to develop the content.

To install MkDocs, use your operating system's package manager:

- Linux: apt-get or yum
- macOS: Homebrew
- Windows: Chocolatey

Because MkDocs is based on Python, you can also install it using the `pip` tool.

Ingredients

- Markdown editor
- MkDocs
- Git (optional)

This recipe goes well with:

- Centralized Git workflow
- GitHub flow

Creating a project

You can create a new doc set just by typing `mkdocs new my-project` and starting to add content. The `mkdocs new` command sets up a directory that contains two things:

- A directory called `docs` containing `index.md`
- A file called `mkdocs.yml` that you use for configuring your project.

As you might have guessed, `index.md` is a congratulatory default first page, and you can change it, add directories and files, and start building the site in the `docs` directory.

HINT: For source control and collaboration, create the project in a Git repo.

Live preview

The command `mkdocs serve` starts a webserver that lets you preview your content as you create it.

NOTE: You must run `mkdocs serve` in the directory that contains the `mkdocs.yml` file.

Whenever you save a Markdown file, MkDocs does its best to update the preview. Sometimes if you change the site navigation, it can't keep up. When that happens, just use Control-C to stop the server and then type the command again to start it.

Here is a screenshot of a Markdown file in Ghostwriter on the left, with the MkDocs preview of the same content on the right.

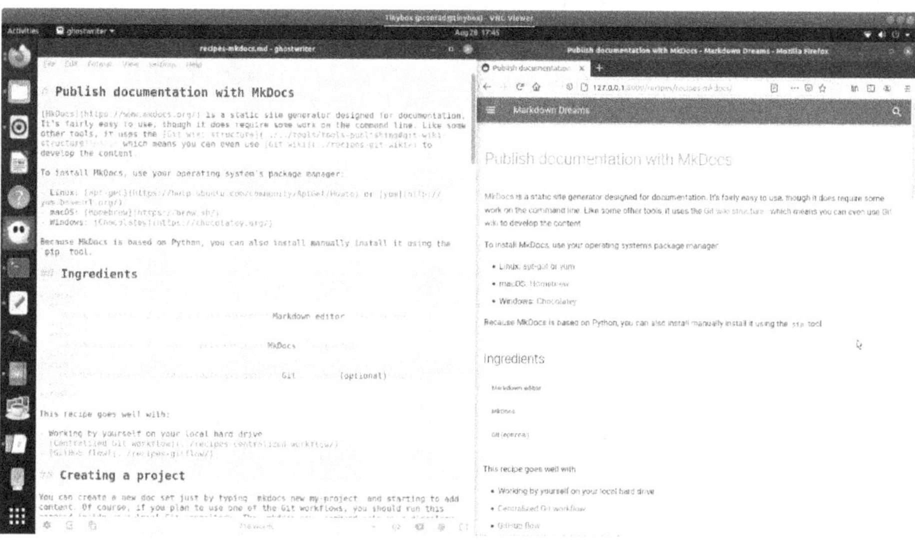

Screenshot of MkDocs live preview

When the webserver starts, it provides information about any broken links in your content, any files that are unused, and where to point your browser to see the content. Here's an abbreviated version of some output I got while working on these recipes:

```
$ mkdocs serve
INFO     -  Building documentation...
INFO     -  Cleaning site directory
INFO     -  The following pages exist in the docs directory,
but are not included in the "nav" configuration:
  - getting-started/index.md
  - recipes/index.md
WARNING -  Documentation file 'recipes/recipes-centralized-
workflow.md' contains a link to 'recipes-slides.md' which i
s not found in the documentation files.
INFO     -  Documentation built in 1.82 seconds
[I 200728 20:45:18 server:296] Serving on http://127.0.0.1:
8000
INFO     -  Serving on http://127.0.0.1:8000
[I 200728 20:45:18 handlers:62] Start watching changes
INFO     -  Start watching changes
[I 200728 20:45:18 handlers:135] Browser Connected: http://
127.0.0.1:8000/recipes/recipes-centralized-workflow/
INFO     -  Browser Connected: http://127.0.0.1:8000/recipes
/recipes-centralized-workflow/
```

Adding a theme

The default look is fine, but you'll probably want to choose a theme.
Themes don't just change the look of the site—they sometimes add
extensions and capabilities (such as the Python Markdown
Extensions). You can find themes by going to the MkDocs site.

To add a theme, you download a bunch of files (sometimes by cloning
a Git repo) and copy them into your MkDocs project directory, then
add the theme name to the theme parameter in the site configuration
file mkdocs.yml.

This file is also where you activate the theme's extensions and set up
site navigation:

- To use the theme's extensions, list them in the
  markdown_extensions parameter
- To set up site navigation, list titles and filenames hierarchically in
  the nav parameter

Here's an abbreviated version of my `mkdocs.yml` file:

```yaml
site_name: Markdown Dreams

theme:
  name: material

markdown_extensions:
  - admonition
  - pymdownx.highlight:
      use_pygments: true
  - pymdownx.snippets
        base_path: 'snippets/'

nav:
    - 'How to do things with Markdown': 'index.md'
    - 'Getting started': 'getting-started/index.md'
    - 'Tools':
        - 'Markdown editors': 'tools/tools-editors.md'
        - 'Source control': 'tools/tools-git.md'
        - 'Publishing': 'tools/tools-publishing.md'
    - 'Recipes':
        - 'Overview': 'recipes/index.md'
        - 'Run a Git wiki': 'recipes/recipes-git-wiki.md'
    - 'Resources': 'resources/index.md'
```

To save length, I stripped out a lot of the navigation, but you get the idea.

HINT: You don't have to set up navigation manually. If you don't, MkDocs provides fairly sensible navigation automatically. But the option is there if you need that level of control.

Working with content

For the most part, working with content is just as you would expect: Markdown in Git wiki structure, using the workflow of your choice. Here are a few tips:

- Links take some getting used to. Each link is relative based on the location of the page in which the link appears. Each file is treated as a folder by the browser. To link to the "Source control" page

from "Run a Git wiki" in the above navigational structure, you would add the following link:
`[Source control](../../tools/tools-git.md)`

- Because all HTML is valid Markdown, you can use HTML. However, you can't use Markdown inside a block of HTML.

- If you choose a theme that includes features like snippets and admonitions, then you can do things outside the bounds of normal Markdown. This is very useful, but makes it harder to use your Markdown source files with other tools (unless you take the fun stuff out).

HINT: If you have trouble with a link or an image, look at the output of `mkdocs serve`.

Snippets

If you use snippets, the location of the included files is relative to the top-level directory of your project (`my-project` for example). It's a good idea to create a directory for snippets and then define it in the `base_path` variable in your `mkdocs.yml` file.

I created a directory called `snippets` and defined it as shown in the `mkdocs.yaml` sample above. That way, I can include snippets using only the filename and I don't have to think about a relative path from the page where I am using the snippet:

HINT: Adding or changing a snippet sometimes requires restarting the webserver before the changes show up in the live preview.

Building and publishing

The `mkdocs build` command builds the website in a directory called `site`.

NOTE: You must run `mkdocs build` in the directory that contains the `mkdocs.yml` file.

To publish the site, use FTP to transfer the contents of that directory to a folder on a webserver.

HINT: To prevent Git from tracking changes to the `site` directory, create a file called `.gitignore` at the top level directory of the MkDocs project with the following contents:

```
site/
```

If you use `git add` to add your `.gitignore` file to change tracking, then it will apply to anyone who clones the repo—meaning that no one will add built HTML pages to Git.

Create a Word document

You can use Pandoc to create a Word document that other people can work on, for upload to Google Drive, or for use with other publishing tools.

Ingredients

- Markdown editor
- Pandoc
- Word, Google Drive, or LibreOffice

Creating the Word document

The command for creating a Word document is simple:

```
pandoc -o my_document.docx my_markdown.md
```

Special Pandoc formatting

Pandoc includes a number of formatting tricks that you might find useful. One of the most useful is fenced div syntax, which uses groups of colons.

You can use fenced div syntax to create columns using nested divs without writing <div> tags in HTML. Take a look at this example:

```
::::::::::::::: {.columns}
::: {.column width="50%"}

Left column:

- Bullet
- Bullet
- Bullet


:::
::: {.column width="50%"}

![](bench.jpg)

:::
:::::::::::::::
```

That translates to a <div class="columns"> containing two <div class="column"> tags. Pandoc uses these to create two columns in the Word doc. Each div can be signified with as few as three colons in a row; in the example, the outer div uses more colons for readability.

You can use curly braces to define attributes such as identifiers, classes, and key/value pairs on headers, images, and a few other elements in Pandoc. If you're using Pandoc to create long Word documents, this is handy because you can set anchors on headings and link to them internally.

You can also use an attribute to scale an image:

```
![Alt text](bench.jpg){width=25%}
```

When Pandoc renders the image, it is scaled to a percentage of the container where it resides (a column, for example). The alt text is used for a caption.

Concatenating multiple files

You can specify as many files as you like. For example:

```
pandoc -o my_document.docx chapter_1.md chapter_2.md
```

Title file

You can specify a title, author, licensing, and other information about the book in a file called `title.txt` at the front of the book, containing YAML that Pandoc uses when it generates the file.

Example:

```
---
title: How to do things with Markdown and Git
author: Peter S. Conrad
language: en-US
...
```

Creating a Word doc with a title file and multiple Markdown files looks like this:

```
pandoc -o my_document.docx title.txt chapt_1.md chapt_2.md
```

Images

When your Markdown includes images, use relative paths. For example:

```
![An image](../images/whatever.png)
```

In the above example, the `images` directory is at the same level as the file containing the Markdown file; the relative path goes up a directory from the Markdown file and then down into the `images` directory to find the image.

When Pandoc follows these relative links, it starts from the directory where you typed the `pandoc` command. If you want Pandoc to find your images, either run the command from a directory where the relative links to the images make sense, or copy the images to a place where the relative links can find them.

Using a reference document

When you use Pandoc to convert Markdown to Word, you can apply the theme and styles from another Word document called a *reference document*. For example:

```
pandoc --reference-doc another.docx -o my_document.docx
```

Cleaning up

If you are converting content from another project—an MkDocs site, for example—the Markdown files might include formatting such as Python extensions that Pandoc doesn't handle. You'll need to edit the PDF and clean up items like admonitions, content tabs, and snippets.

Create an ePub book

You can use Pandoc to create an ePub book suitable for tablets and phones or for self-publishing on Amazon.

Ingredients

- Markdown editor
- Pandoc
- An ePub editor such as Sigil

Creating the book

The command for creating an ePub book is simple:

```
pandoc -o my_book.epub my_markdown.md
```

Concatenating multiple files

You can specify as many files as you like. For example:

```
pandoc -o my_book.epub chapter_1.md chapter_2.md
```

Title file

You can specify a title, author, licensing, and other information about the book in a file called `title.txt` at the front of the book, containing YAML that Pandoc uses when it generates the ePub file.

Example:

```
---
title: How to do things with Markdown and Git
author: Peter S. Conrad
language: en-US
...
```

Creating a book with a title file and multiple Markdown files looks like this:

```
pandoc -o my_book.epub title.txt chapter_1.md chapter_2.md
```

Images

When your book includes images, use relative paths. For example:

```
![An image](../images/whatever.png)
```

In the above example, the `images` directory is at the same level as the file containing the Markdown file; the relative path goes up a directory from the Markdown file and then down into the `images` directory to find the image.

When Pandoc follows these relative links, it starts from the directory where you typed the `pandoc` command. If you want Pandoc to find your images, either run the command from a directory where the relative links to the images make sense, or copy the images to a place where the relative links can find them.

Cleaning up

If you are converting content from another project—an MkDocs site, for example—the Markdown files might include formatting such as Python extensions that Pandoc doesn't handle. You'll need to edit the ePub and clean up items like admonitions, content tabs, and snippets.

Working with a large number of files

When your book contains many files, the command can get unwieldy:

```
pandoc -o markdown-dreams.epub title.txt ../index.md ../get
ting-started/getting-started.md ../tools/tools-editors.md .
./tools/tools-storage.md ../tools/tools-git.md ../tools/too
ls- git-setup.md ../tools/tools-git-basics.md ../tools/tool
s-publishing.md ../recipes/recipes-notes.md ../recipes/reci
pes-git-wiki.md ../recipes/recipes-centralized-workflow.md
../recipes/recipes-gitflow.md ../recipes/recipes-hugo.md ..
/recipes/recipes-mkdocs.md ../recipes/recipes-pandoc-word.m
d ../recipes/recipes-pandoc-ebook.md ../recipes/recipes-pan
doc-pdf.md ../recipes/recipes-pandoc-web.md ../recipes/reci
pes-slides.md ../recipes/recipes-slides-dzslides.md ../reci
pes/recipes-slides-remark.md ../resources/markdown-cheatshe
et.md ../resources/resources-glossary.md ../resources/templ
ates.md ../resources/links.md
```

With a lot of chapters, you will find it easier to use a script. You can run the script by typing a single command, and you can edit the script easily to make changes. You can create a script on macOS or Linux, or using the new Bash shell in Windows 10.

Here is an example:

```
#!/bin/bash

pandoc -o markdown-dreams.epub \
    title.txt \
    ../index.md \
    ../getting-started/getting-started.md \
    ../tools/tools-editors.md \
    ../tools/tools-storage.md \
    ../tools/tools-git.md \
    ../tools/tools-git-setup.md \
    ../tools/tools-git-basics.md \
    ../tools/tools-publishing.md \
    ../recipes/recipes-notes.md \
    ../recipes/recipes-git-wiki.md \
    ../recipes/recipes-centralized-workflow.md \
    ../recipes/recipes-gitflow.md \
    ../recipes/recipes-hugo.md \
    ../recipes/recipes-mkdocs.md \
    ../recipes/recipes-pandoc-word.md \
    ../recipes/recipes-pandoc-ebook.md \
    ../recipes/recipes-pandoc-pdf.md \
    ../recipes/recipes-pandoc-web.md \
    ../recipes/recipes-slides.md .\
    ../recipes/recipes-slides-dzslides.md \
    ../recipes/recipes-slides-remark.md \
    ../resources/markdown-cheatsheet.md \
    ../resources/resources-glossary.md \
    ../resources/templates.md \
    ../resources/links.md
```

The first line tells the computer that this is a Bash script. After that, you can just type the command the same way you would run it on the command line. For readability (and ease of editing), you can break likes with a backslash.

Save the file with a short name like `build.sh` and make it executable. At the command prompt, you can type:

```
chmod +x build.sh
```

You can then run the script by name:

```
./build.sh
```

Create a PDF

You can use Pandoc to create a PDF, which is a pleasant way to share content that you don't want other people to edit along the way.

Ingredients

- Markdown editor
- Pandoc
- Adobe Acrobat

Creating the PDF

The command for creating a PDF is simple:

```
pandoc -o my_document.pdf my_markdown.md
```

Concatenating multiple files

You can specify as many files as you like. For example:

```
pandoc -o my_document.pdf chapt_1.md chapt_2.md
```

Title file

You can specify a title, author, licensing, and other information about the book in a file called `title.txt` at the front of the book, containing YAML that Pandoc uses when it generates the PDF file.

Example:

```
---
title: How to do things with Markdown and Git
author: Peter S. Conrad
language: en-US
...
```

Creating a PDF with a title file and multiple Markdown files looks like this:

```
pandoc -o my_document.pdf title.txt chapt_1.md chapt_2.md
```

Images

When your Markdown includes images, use relative paths. For example:

```
![An image](../images/whatever.png)
```

In the above example, the images directory is at the same level as the file containing the Markdown file; the relative path goes up a directory from the Markdown file and then down into the images directory to find the image.

When Pandoc follows these relative links, it starts from the directory where you typed the pandoc command. If you want Pandoc to find your images, either run the command from a directory where the relative links to the images make sense, or copy the images to a place where the relative links can find them.

Errors

Pandoc can use a number of different PDF engines with different capabilities. In some cases, special characters or other formatting can cause the PDF creation to fail. You can try specifying a different PDF engine, remove the characters or formatting causing the problem, or create a Word document and export the PDF from there.

Cleaning up

If you are converting content from another project—an MkDocs site, for example—the Markdown files might contain formatting such as Python extensions that Pandoc doesn't handle. You'll need to edit the PDF and clean up items like admonitions, content tabs, and snippets.

Grab a web page with Pandoc

Converting a web page to Markdown on the fly is a small task that can be very helpful if you need to grab content for editing or add information from the web to your notes.

Ingredients

- Markdown editor
- Pandoc

Syntax

The command is simple:

```
pandoc -s -r html <URL> -o <Markdown filename>
```

Example:

```
pandoc -s -r html http://www.example.com/ -o markdown.md
```

Result

The result is a Markdown file converted from the web page. Because most modern web pages include a lot of code in addition to the human-readable content, you might have to do a little cleanup. However, you can see that the content is easy to read and convenient to copy and paste to another Markdown file. Pandoc tries its best to convert the `<div>` tags and their attributes to its own fenced div notation, which makes even the extra junk more readable as well.

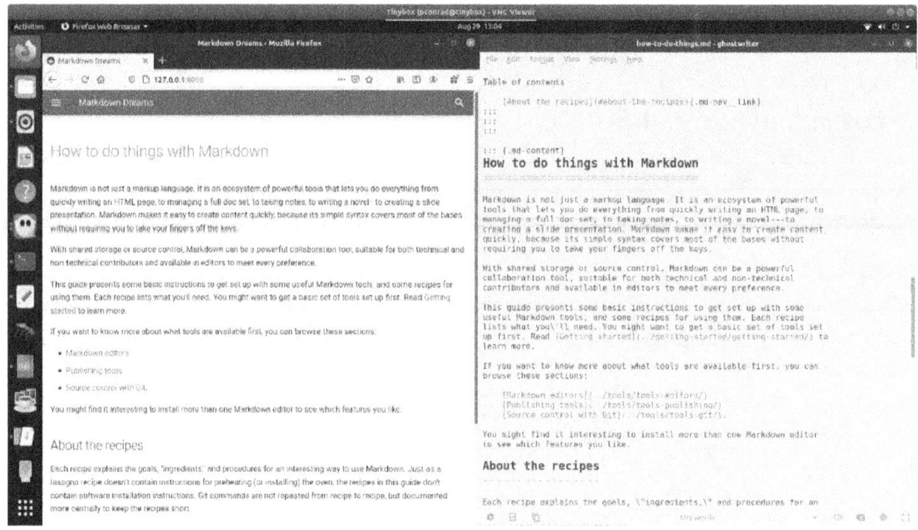

Create a PowerPoint presentation

You can use Pandoc to create a presentation for display and editing in PowerPoint, for upload to Google Drive, or for use with other publishing tools.

Ingredients

Markdown editor

Pandoc

PowerPoint, Google Drive, or LibreOffice

Markdown for PowerPoint slides

Start your Markdown file with YAML metadata or a simple block like this:

```
% Title
% Author Name
% Date
```

Pandoc uses a complicated rule to figure out what header level to use for slide titles, but it boils down to this:

- Use heading level one (#) for a section title
- Use heading level two (##) for a slide title

For example:

```
# Section Title

## Slide Title

Text on a slide:

* Bullet
* Bullet
* Bullet

::: notes
Speaker notes go here
:::
```

The above Markdown contains two slides:

- A section title slide
- A slide with a level two heading for the title

Notice the ::: characters—this is Pandoc's fenced div syntax, which lets you do a lot of tricks in various formats. Here, it is just used to delineate the speaker notes.

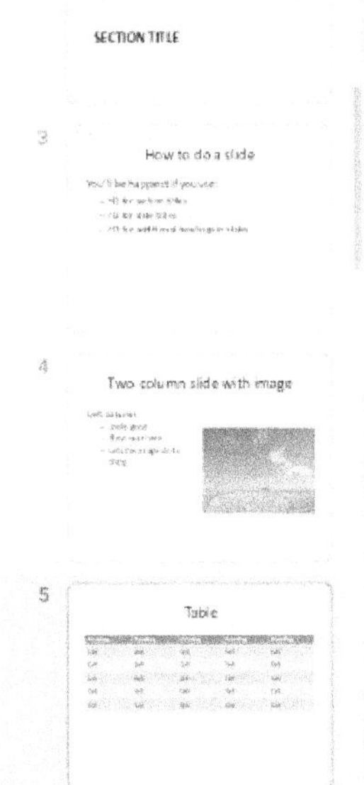

Special Pandoc formatting

Pandoc includes a number of formatting tricks that you might find useful. One of the most useful is fenced div syntax, which uses groups of colons as shorthand for `<div>` tags.

Take a look at this example:

```
:::::::::::::::: {.columns}
::: {.column width="50%"}

Left column:

- Bullet
- Bullet
- Bullet

:::
::: {.column width="50%"}

![](bench.jpg)

:::
::::::::::::::::
```

That translates to a `<div class="columns">` tag containing two `<div class="column">` tags. Pandoc uses these to create two columns in a PowerPoint slide. Each div can be signified with as few as three colons in a row. In the example, the outer div uses more colons for readability.

The curly braces let you define *attributes* such as identifiers, classes, and key/value pairs on headers, images, and a few other elements in Pandoc. In the above example, the attributes specify the names and widths of the divs.

Images

When your Markdown includes images, use relative paths. For example:

```
![An image](../images/whatever.png)
```

In the above example, the `images` directory is at the same level as the file containing the Markdown file; the relative path goes up a directory from the Markdown file and then down into the `images` directory to find the image.

When Pandoc follows these relative links, it starts from the directory where you typed the `pandoc` command. If you want Pandoc to find your images, either run the command from a directory where the relative links to the images make sense, or copy the images to a place where the relative links can find them.

You can use an attribute to scale an image:

```
![An image](bench.jpg){width=25%}
```

When Pandoc renders the image, it is scaled to a percentage of the container where it resides (a column, for example). The alt text is used for a caption.

Creating the presentation

The command for creating the document is simple. With a single
Markdown file, it looks like this:

```
pandoc -o my_slides.pptx my_slides.md
```

Using a reference document

You can apply the theme and styles from another PowerPoint
document called a *reference document.* For example:

```
pandoc --reference-doc my_doc.pptx -o slides.pptx slides.md
```

This gives your converted PowerPoint document the same look and
feel as the other presentation.

Create a DZSlides presentation

You can use Pandoc to create a standalone slide presentation in DZSlides format, which is useful for presenting when you aren't sure what software will be available. DZSlides creates bold, attractive slides that discourage the use of too much text.

Ingredients

- Markdown editor
- Pandoc
- A browser

Markdown for DZSlides

Start your Markdown file with YAML metadata or a block like this:

```
% Title
% Author Name
% Date
```

DZSlides uses the horizontal rule (---) as a separator between slides. A level one or level two heading is a section title.

Here's some sample Markdown:

```
---

# H1 or H2 is a Section Title

---

Normal Text or Slide Title

- Bullet
- Bullet

---

Normal text is big enough for a title or announcement on a
slide.
```

How to do a slide

- Use --- to separate slides
- Use regular text and bullets
- H1 or H2 for a section title

The layout of slides in DZslides is simple; you probably won''t find yourself using tables or columns a lot.

Images

When your Markdown includes images, use relative paths. For example:

```
![An image](../images/whatever.png)
```

In the above example, the `images` directory is at the same level as the file containing the Markdown file; the relative path goes up a directory from the Markdown file and then down into the `images` directory to find the image.

When Pandoc follows these relative links, it starts from the directory where you typed the `pandoc` command. If you want Pandoc to find your images, either run the command from a directory where the relative links to the images make sense, or copy the images to a place where the relative links can find them.

After you create the presentation, which is an HTML file, you need to keep the images and the presentation together. If you copy your presentation to a thumb drive without the images, the images won't work.

HINT: It's a good idea to create the Markdown presentation in a folder with all the images it needs, then use Pandoc to build the presentation in the same folder. You can copy the entire folder wherever you need it, knowing that all the images for the presentation will work.

Pandoc provides syntax for scaling an image:

```
![An image](bench.jpg){width=25%}
```

When Pandoc renders the image, it is scaled to a percentage of the container where it resides (the slide, in most cases). The alt text is used for a caption.

Creating the presentation

The command for creating the document is simple. With a single Markdown file, it looks like this:

```
pandoc -t dzslides -s myslides.md -o myslides.htm
```

The -s option tells Pandoc to create a standalone presentation, including all the CSS, HTML, and JavaScript needed to display it. You can view the presentation by opening the resulting HTML file in a browser.

Create a Remark presentation

Remark is a standalone slide presentation tool that you edit directly and view in a browser. You create slides in your favorite Markdown editor, then paste them into a specific place in the HTML file.

There are three ways to use Remark:

- `boilerplate-single.html` – a standalone presentation containing the entire JavaScript code
- `boilerplate-local.html` – a standalone presentation that references the JavaScript code from a local file
- `boilerplate-remote.html` – a presentation that references the JavaScript code online

You can find these versions of Remark by going to *remarkjs.com*.

HINT: If you're not sure which version to choose, start with `boilerplate-remote.html` because it is easy to edit and doesn't require you to download the JavaScript file separately.

Ingredients

- Markdown editor
- Remark.js
- A browser

Markdown for Remark

Remark uses level one or level two headings for slide titles and separates slides with the horizontal rule (---). Speaker notes are at the end of each slide, marked by three question marks (???).

Here is some example Markdown:

```
class: center, middle

# Remark template
.right[Author]
.right[Date]

---

# Slide title

Normal text:

* Bullet
* Bullet
* Bullet

???
Speaker notes go here

---
```

Remark provides some CSS to style slides. The above example uses
`class: center, middle` to put the slide title in the middle of the
slide, and `.right` to align the text showing the author and date.

You can use normal Markdown image syntax, but you can also use CSS
and HTML to change the way images appear:

```
.center[<img src="bench.jpg" width=50% height=50%></img>]
```

Images

You can use CSS and HTML to do images:

More complicated CSS is available if you want to experiment further, but is beyond the scope of this recipe.

Creating the presentation

Remark needs three things to work: boilerplate HTML, the `remark.js` script, and your Markdown.

1. Open boilerplate-remote.html in a text editor.
2. Add your Markdown in the `source` text area. Example:

```
<textarea id="source">
class: center, middle

# Title

---

# Agenda

1. Introduction
2. Deep-dive
3. ...

---

# Introduction

</textarea>
```

3. Save the file with a new name (`my-slides.html`, for example) and open it in a browser.

Any changes you save from the text editor show up in the browser when you reload. Like other browser-based slide tools, remember that you need to keep your images where the HTML expects to find them.

HINT: It's a good idea to create the Markdown in a folder together with the boilerplate HTML, any images, and `remark.js` (if needed). That way, you can copy the entire folder wherever you need it, knowing that the presentation will work.

Markdown cheatsheet

Headers
```
# H1
## H2
### H3
#### H4
##### H5
###### H6
```

Line breaks and paragraphs
```
Consecutive lines
of any length
run together and become a single paragraph.
```
Consecutive lines of any length run together and become a single paragraph.

```
An empty line ends the paragraph and starts a new
one.
```

```
Two spaces at the end of a line
Forces a line break without
Starting a new paragraph.
```

Text effects
```
*emphasis* (italics)
_emphasis_ (italics)
**strong** (bold)
__strong__ (bold)
**combined _emphasis_**
`code`
~~strikethrough~~
```

Lists

Bullet list:

```
* Asterisks, plus signs, or minus signs

  Indent two spaces to add another paragraph in a
  list item
* Another list item
```

Numbered list:

```
1. The numbers don't matter.
1. Markdown numbers when it renders
```

```
   Indent three spaces to add another paragraph
   in a list item
1. Lists inside lists:

   * Ordered and unordered lists work
```

Links

You can define links inline or by reference. Reference links have a label—text or a number, like this: [1]

```
This is an
[inline-style link](https://www.example.com).
A link can have a
[title](https://www.example.com "Example title").
Links can be defined later by [reference][label].

    ...

[label]:
https://www.example.com/any/label/text/is/fine
```

Images

You define an image just like a link, but with an exclamation mark.

Inline:

```
![alt text](https://www.example.com/image.png)
```

Reference:

```
![alt text][label text]

    ...

[label text]: https://www.example.com/image.png
```

Code blocks

There are two ways to create code blocks, both of which can be embedded in lists.

```
In standard Markdown, indent by 4 spaces:

    10 PRINT "HELLO"
    20 GOTO 10
```

```
Many Markdown flavors provide the capability to
do a fenced code block,
surrounded by three backticks. You can indicate
the language for syntax
highlighting:

``` basic

10 PRINT "HELLO"
20 GOTO 10

```
```

Blockquotes

```
> Use a greater-than sign plus a space at the
beginning of a paragraph.
You can add it to the start of every line, or
just the first line in the
paragraph.

> But it looks better to put it at the start of
every line. This makes it
> easier to see which lines are part of the
blockquote.
```

Tables

Some flavors of Markdown include simple table syntax. Default alignment is left. Colons indicate other column alignments.

```
| Header       | Row is       | mandatory      |
| ------------ |:------------:| -------------:|
| Cell         | Cell         | Cell           |
```

Horizontal rule

Three ways to add a horizontal rule—three or more hyphens, asterisks, or underscores:

```
---

***

___
```

Comments

There are two ways to write comments: HTML-style comments, which are rendered as part of the HTML source code, and two kinds of link-style comments that are a bit of a hack and don't get rendered at all.

```
<!-- HTML-style comments -->
  are visible in Markdown and in rendered HTML.

[//]: # "This comment"
  is only visible in the Markdown and doesn't get
rendered.

[comment]: <> "This comment"
  is only visible in the Markdown and doesn't get
    rendered.
```

HTML and special characters

HTML is part of Markdown. You can use HTML to insert tables, formatting, special characters, and other features that Markdown doesn't support directly. HTML tables are often better and easier than Markdown tables. You can escape characters with a backslash (\) or use HTML codes:

```
&mdash; em-dash
&ndash; en-dash
&#35; octothorpe
&#42; asterisk
```

Templates

Use these templates as starting points for slide presentations.

DZSlides

Save this text as a Markdown file, then use Pandoc to convert it to a DZSlides presentation.

% DZslides template for Pandoc
% Peter Conrad
% 26 November 2020

Section titles

- H1 or H2
- Centered on slide
- Not much room below

<!--
   An H1 or H2 renders as a large title in the middle of the
slide.
   There is room for a small number of bullets below, but it
looks
   nicer with the title alone.
-->

How to do a slide

- Use \-\-\- to separate slides
- Use regular text and bullets
- H1 or H2 for a section title

<!--
   Regular text starts closer to the top of the slide.
   A normal text phrase plus bullets makes for a simple,
   attractive slide.
-->

Images

You can use images.

  - Provide width and height
  - Keep them with the HTML file

```
![](bench.jpg){width=33% height=33%}

<!--
  If you omit width and height, the images tend to
  appear pixel-for-pixel at the resolution of the screen.
  This often means: very huge. Pandoc can resize the
  images for you.

  Remember that you need to keep the image files with your
  presentation's HTML file or they won't show up.
-->


---


![Full-screen image with alt text](bench.jpg){width=100% he
ight=100%}

<!--
  For some reason, a full-screen image renders properly eve
n if
  you omit the width and height tags. I have left them in t
o foster
  good habits.
-->


---


# Columns


---


::::::::::::::: {.columns}
::: {.column width="50%"}
Columns work



:::
::: {.column width="50%"}
**Lists** in columns don't work
![](../path/to/image.jpg){width=100% height=100%}
<!-- 100% of this column, that is -->
:::
```

::::::::::::::::

```
<!--
  Pandoc supports multiple columns in slide shows.
  I get the impression that DZslides is designed to create
  a slide show with a very simple, uncluttered look.
  If you are using a lot of columns, you might consider
  a different slide format.
-->
```

Syntax

Emphasis

- **bold**
- *italic*
- **_both_**
- ~~strike~~

> Blockquotes look like this

Lists

- Bullets work
  -   Indenting works
- Ordered lists don't
  - By themselves, they go to the left edge
  - As a sub-list, they outdent to the next level

Incremental "build" slides

::: incremental

- Incremental slides work
- This is how they look
- It's fine

:::

A slide with a pause can work.

. . .

Or can it?

Tables work but they are not well padded and they are stuck
at the top left of the slide.

Don't use inline code or code blocks. They don't look quite
right.

Thank you

PowerPoint

Save this as a Markdown file and then use Pandoc to convert it to a PowerPoint presentation.

```
% Pandoc Template for Powerpoint
% Peter Conrad
% 22 November 2020

# Section Title


## How to do a slide

You'll be happiest if you use:

* H1 for section titles
- H2 for slide titles
+ H3 for additional headings in slides

::: notes

Speaker notes go here

:::

## Two-column slide with image


:::::::::::::::: {.columns}
::: {.column width="50%"}
Left column:

- Looks good
- Stays over here
- Lets the image do its thing
:::
::: {.column width="50%"}
![](bench.jpg)
:::
::::::::::::::::

::: notes

Speaker notes go here

:::
```

Table

Heading	Heading	Heading	Heading	Heading
Cell	Cell	Cell	Cell	Cell
Cell	Cell	Cell	Cell	Cell
Cell	Cell	Cell	Cell	Cell
Cell	Cell	Cell	Cell	Cell
Cell	Cell	Cell	Cell	Cell

::: notes

Speaker notes go here

:::

Limitations

Things that don't work

- HTML in your Markdown
- CSS
- Builds
  - (pauses or incremental lists)
- Inline monospace

::: notes

Speaker notes go here

:::

Things that work very well

- Images resize nicely (but don't fill the screen)
- Tables look nice
- You don't have to take your images with you

::: notes

Speaker notes go here

:::

An image

`![Alt text looks like this](../path/to/image.jpg){width=25% }`

::: notes

Speaker notes go here

:::

Headings

Headings H3 and lower look the same.

H3
H4
H5
H6

::: notes

Speaker notes go here

:::

Emphasis

- **bold**
- *italic*
- **_both_**
- ~~strike~~

::: notes
Speaker notes go here
:::

Bullet lists

- Bullets work
  -   Indenting works
- Don't try to do multiple lists on a single slide

Ordered lists

1. Ordered lists work
   1. Sub-lists in ordered lists
1. Next item

::: notes
Speaker notes go here
:::

Remark

Copy and paste this template between the opening and closing `<textarea id="source">` tags in the Remark boilerplate HTML.

```
class: center, middle

# Title

---

# Agenda

1. Introduction
2. Deep-dive
3. ...

---

# Introduction

---

# Text alignment

.left[Left-aligned text]

.center[Centered text]

.right[Right-aligned text]

???
Speaker notes go here

---

# Images

You can use CSS and HTML to do images:

.center[<img src="bench.jpg" width=50% height=50%></img>]

---

background-image: url(bench.jpg)
background-size: contain
```

```
# Slide with background image

---

# Incremental slide

- You build bullet lists like this

--

- with two-dash separators

???
Speaker notes go here

--

{{content}}
- Incrementally

???
Speaker notes go here

--

- And with the \{\{content}} directive you can say where th
e next piece of content should go.

---

class: center, middle

# Thank you
```

Glossary

admonition
A note, warning, or other call-out that draws attention to a block of content.

Bash
A Unix/Linux shell and language that lets users execute commands and programs.

branch
A series of commits representing changes to one or more files in a Git repository.

change
In Git, a modification, creation, or deletion of a file.

checkout
In Git, to switch to a different branch or restore a file.

chmod
A shell command that changes file permissions.

client
Hardware or software that accesses a *service*. A web browser is a client to a webserver, and a Git client accesses a service provided by a Git host.

clone
In Git, to make a complete local copy of a *remote repository* so you can work with the files on your computer.

cloud
Someone else's computer.

commit
In Git, to save your changes to the *local repository*.

A group of changes saved together using the `commit` command.

CSS
Cascading Style Sheets, a style sheet language for defining the look and feel of a document written in HTML or another markup language.

div
A division or section in an HTML document, specified with a `<div>` tag.

dynamic site
A site that is generated or modified at the time it is displayed. See *static site.*

fenced
Delineated with a series of characters. For example, a *fenced code block* is marked with three backticks (```) at the top and bottom.

frontmatter
Metadata at the start of a file, often including information such as the title, author, and date.

FTP
File Transfer Protocol, a way of exchanging files between your computer and a server.

Git
A distributed source control system.

Git wiki
An additional repository, attached to a Git repository, for the purpose of displaying and managing content (often, content about the Git repository).

Git wiki structure
A content structure in which the display paths or URLs to content pages are defined by the directory paths of the files that make up the content.

host
A server, often on the web. A *Git host* provides access to Git repositories, a *web host* provides access to websites, and so on.

HTML
HyperText Markup Language, the standard markup language for creating web pages.

JavaScript
A programming language that enables the creation of interactive features on web pages.

JSON
JavaScript Object Notation, a format for storing and transporting data.

LaTeX
A document preparation system for high-quality typesetting.

Linux
A family of Unix-like operating systems first designed by Linus Torvalds in 1991.

local
On your own computer.

Markdown
A simple *markup language* originally designed as an easy way to write HTML pages.

markup language
A way of indicating display formatting and other information within a document.

merge
In Git, to combine two sets of changes into one branch.

merge conflict
In Git, a merge that cannot be completed automatically because the same parts of the files have been modified in both sets of changes.

metadata
Information about the content in a file, or about the file itself.

package manager
A tool for installing software. See Getting started.

PDF
Portable Document Format, a file format developed by Adobe in 1993 to present documents consistently across software, hardware, and operating systems.

permissions
Settings that specify what actions can be taken and by whom. For example, file permissions can specify who can read, write, or execute the file.

pull
In Git, to fetch and merge changes from a *remote* to your *local repository*.

pull request
In Git, a set of proposed changes to be approved and then merged into a branch.

push
In Git, to upload changes from your local *repository* to a *remote*.

Python
A popular programming language.

Python Markdown extensions
A set of additional features and syntax provided with the Python implementation of Markdown.

recursion
See *recursion*.

remote
A *remote repository*.

remote repository
A version of your project that is hosted on the network or online rather than on your computer.

repo
Repository.

repository
In Git, a collection of files and the entire history of all changes made to them.

Samba
Open source software that runs on Unix or Linux to enable communication with Windows clients over a network.

script
A computer program that automates the execution of commands or tasks.

server
A computer or application that provides a service for other programs or devices, which in turn are called *clients*.

Sharepoint
A web-based collaboratoin platform that integrates with Microsoft Office and is often used to manage and store documents.

shell
A program that lets users type commands for the operating system to execute.

source control
A way of tracking and managing changes to code or other content.

stage
In Git, to specify which changes to save in the next *commit*.

stash
In Git, to record the current state of the working directory and revert the working directory to the previous *commit*.

static site
A site composed of HTML pages or other documents that are made available exactly as stored, as opposed to a *dynamic site* whose pages are rendered on the fly when they are requested. A static site often performs better and can be more secure, but lacks some of the capabilities of a *dynamic site*.

static site generator
A tool that builds a *static site*.

TOML
Tom's Obvious, Minimal Language, a text format for configuration files or metadata.

Unix
A family of operating systems designed at Bell Labs in the 1970s, that Linux is like.

unstage
In Git, to remove previously *staged* changes from the upcoming *commit.*

WebDAV
Web Distributed Authoring and Versioning, an HTTP extension that lets clients perform remote operations on content.

wiki
A structured HTML site, often edited and managed by the readers themselves, that collects information about a particular topic.

working branch
In Git, a temporary branch created for working on a particular set of content or code changes.

working directory
The folder on your local computer where you store the content you are editing.

WYSIWYG
What You See Is What You Get, an editing experience that mimics the appearance of the document in its final form.

YAML
Yaml Ain't Markup Language, a text format for configuration files or metadata.

Links

Editors

- Atom - https://atom.io/
- BbEdit - https://www.barebones.com/products/bbedit/bb
- Byword - https://bywordapp.com/
- Caret - https://caret.io/
- Dillinger - https://dillinger.io/
- Emacs - https://www.gnu.org/software/emacs/
- Ghostwriter - https://wereturtle.github.io/ghostwriter/
- HackMD – https://hackmd.io/
- iA Writer - https://ia.net/writer
- Joplin - https://joplinapp.org/
- MacDown - https://macdown.uranusjr.com/
- Mou - http://25.io/mou/
- StackEdit - https://stackedit.io/
- Sublime Text - https://www.sublimetext.com/
- Typora - https://typora.io/
- Vim - https://www.vim.org/
- Visual Studio Code - https://code.visualstudio.com/

Git

- Bitbucket - https://bitbucket.org/
- Dangit, Git!?! - https://dangitgit.com/
- Git - https://git-scm.com/
- Git doesn't have to be hard https://levelup.gitconnected.com/git-doesnt-have-to-be-hard-e1e115be6668
- GitHub - https://bitbucket.org/
- GitHub Desktop - https://desktop.github.com/
- GitHub Flow - https://scottchacon.com/2011/08/31/github-flow.html
- GitLab - https://about.gitlab.com/
- Git Wikis - https://docs.gitlab.com/ee/user/project/wiki/
- Sourcetree - https://www.sourcetreeapp.com/

* The Git Book - https://git-scm.com/book/en/v2

Markdown

* Babelmark - https://babelmark.github.io/
* CommonMark - https://commonmark.org/
* GitHub Flavored Markdown (GFM) - https://github.github.com/gfm/
* Markdown - https://www.markdownguide.org/basic-syntax/
* Markdown Dingus - https://daringfireball.net/projects/markdown/dingus
* Markdown Extra - https://michelf.ca/projects/php-markdown/extra/
* Markdown+Math - https://marketplace.visualstudio.com/items?itemName=goessner.mdmath
* Mermaid - https://mermaid-js.github.io/mermaid/#/
* MultiMarkdown (MMD) - https://fletcherpenney.net/multimarkdown/
* Python Markdown Extensions - https://python-markdown.github.io/extensions/
* Why you should and should not use Markdown https://www.youtube.com/watch?v=Z2ZXL_TdINA

Tools

* Acrobat - https://get.adobe.com/reader/
* Amazon bookshelf - https://kdp.amazon.com/en_US/bookshelf
* apt-get - https://help.ubuntu.com/community/AptGet/Howto
* Blogger - https://www.blogger.com/
* Box - https://www.box.com/
* Chocolatey - https://chocolatey.org/
* DropBox - https://www.dropbox.com/
* DZSlides - http://paulrouget.com/dzslides/
* FileZilla - https://filezilla-project.org/
* gFTP - https://en.wikipedia.org/wiki/GFTP
* Homebrew - https://brew.sh/

- Hugo – https://gohugo.io/
    - Themes - https://themes.gohugo.io/
- LibreOffice - https://www.libreoffice.org/
- Medium - https://medium.com/
- Microsoft Office - https://www.office.com/
- MkDocs – https://www.mkdocs.org/
    - Themes - https://github.com/mkdocs/mkdocs/wiki/MkDocs-Themes
- OneDrive - https://onedrive.live.com/
- Pandoc - https://pandoc.org/
    - Try it online - https://pandoc.org/try/
- Remark - https://remarkjs.com/#1
- Sigil - https://sigil-ebook.com/
- Transmit - https://panic.com/transmit/
- Wordpress - https://wordpress.com/
- yum - http://yum.baseurl.org/